THE CENTRALITY OF THE RESUR- RECTION

ERRATUM

Several pages in the Conclusion (pp. 135-43) are out of order. The proper page sequence should be: 137, 140, 141, 138, 139, 142. . . .

THE CENTRALITY OF THE RESURRECTION

A Study in Paul's Soteriology

Richard B. Gaffin, Jr.

BAKER BOOK HOUSE
Grand Rapids, Michigan

Copyright 1978 by
Baker Book House Company
ISBN: 0-8010-3726-3
Library of Congress Catalog Card Number: 78-057894
Printed in the United States of America

In memory of

Geerhardus Vos

Professor of Biblical Theology,
Princeton Theological Seminary (1893-1932)

and

John Murray

Professor of Systematic Theology,
Westminster Theological Seminary (1930-1966)

"To take God as source and end of all that exists and happens, and to hold such a view suffused with the warmth of genuine devotion, stands not only related to theology as the fruit stands to the tree: it is by reason of its essence a veritable theological tree of life."

Contents

Preface 9

Abbreviations 10

Introduction 11

PART ONE

Methodological Considerations 17

PART TWO

*The Resurrection of Christ in Paul's Soteriology:
The Central Theme and Basic Structure* ....

The Resurrection of Christ and the Future Resurrection of
Believers 31

  I Corinthians 15:20ff 33
  Colossians 1:18 34
  I Corinthians 15:12-19 36
  II Corinthians 4:14 39

The Resurrection of Christ and the Past Resurrection of the
Believer 41

  Ephesians 2:5, 6 41
  Colossians 2:12, 13; 3:1 43
  Romans 6:3ff. 44
  Galatians 2:19, 20 52
  The Union Involved 53
  Summary and Conclusions 58

Conclusion 59

The Activity of the Father and the Passivity of the Son 62

The Agency of the Spirit 66

  Romans 8:11 66

The Spirit, Glory, Power, and Life 68
The Person of the Spirit 70

Conclusion 74

PART THREE

The Resurrection of Christ in Paul's Soteriology:
The Development of the Theme 75

The Resurrection of Christ 78

I Corinthians 15:45 78
II Corinthians 3:17 92
Romans 1:3, 4 98
Acts 13:33 113
The Resurrection As the Redemption of Christ 114

Adoption 117
Justification 119
Sanctification 124
Glorification 126
Conclusion 127

Raised With Christ 127

CONCLUSION 135

Selected Bibliography 145
Scripture Index 147
Author Index 151
Subject Index 155

Preface

This study, under the title *Resurrection and Redemption: A Study in Pauline Soteriology* (University Microfilms, Ann Arbor, Michigan; order number: 70-10, 417), was originally presented to the faculty of Westminster Theological Seminary in partial fulfillment of the requirements for the degree of Doctor of Theology in 1969. It has been thoroughly rewritten for publication but with only minor alterations in substance. Foreign language quotations from secondary sources have been put into English. Occasionally, references in footnotes to works in foreign languages or to works no longer accessible to the average reader have been deleted. Use of the original biblical languages has been kept to a minimum and, where included, should not keep the reader who is unfamiliar with these languages from following the discussion. The bibliography has been significantly condensed.

The relevant literature which has appeared in the meantime does not, in my judgment, require substantial changes in the work as a whole. I am keenly aware of the tentativeness of some points made in the conclusion and the need to expand and clarify them. But such an expansion is better served by a study of its own.

Part I has appeared with some alterations in *Jerusalem and Athens: Critical Discussions on the Theology and Apologetics of Cornelius Van Til*, edited by E. R. Geehan (Presbyterian and Reformed, 1971), pp. 228-237.

My thanks to Mrs. Betty Stevenson and Miss Dorothy Krieke for their work in typing the manuscript.

RICHARD B. GAFFIN, JR.
Westminster Theological Seminary
December 1977

Abbreviations

ATANT	*Abhandlungen zur Theologie des Alten und Neuen Testaments*, ed. W. Eichrodt and O. Cullmann
CNT	*Commentaar op het Nieuwe Testament*, S.Greijdanus and F. W. Grosheide, founders
ICC	*The International Critical Commentary*
KNT	*Kommentaar op het Nieuwe Testament*, ed. S. Greijdanus and F. W. Grosheide
MeyerK	*Kritisch-exegetischer Kommentar über das Neue Testament*, H. A. W. Meyer, founder
NA	*Neutestamentliche Abhandlungen*
NICNT	*New International Commentary on the New Testament*, ed. N. B. Stonehouse and F. F. Bruce
NTD	*Das Neue Testament Deutsch*, ed. P. Althaus and G. Friedrich
SBT	*Studies in Biblical Theology*
TDNT	*Theological Dictionary of the New Testament*, trans. G. W. Bromiley, vols. 1-4, ed. G. Kittel, vols. 5-7 ed. G. Friedrich, Grand Rapids: Eerdmans, 1964ff.
WTJ	*The Westminster Theological Journal*
ZahnK	*Kommentar zum Neuen Testament*, ed. Theodor Zahn
ZTK	*Zeitschrift für Theologie und Kirche*

Introduction

Biblical interpretation never takes place in a vacuum. A variety of contextual elements on the side of the interpreter inevitably come into play, exerting a decided, if not always recognized, control. Two factors especially shape the overall direction of this study and significantly influence its emphases.

(1) Reformed theology has always thought itself to be distinctively Pauline, more sensitive than other traditions to the deeper motives and trends of the apostle's teaching and more consistent in its expression of them. In the course of its development, however, it has not found particular *dogmatic* significance in Paul's statements regarding Jesus' resurrection. The convergence of two factors explains this state of affairs. On the one hand, Paul's distinguishing interest has been seen to lie in the area of soteriology, i.e., the application of redemption to the individual believer. Forensic aspects, the doctrine of justification by faith in particular, have been judged to be central. In other words, access to the structure of Paul's teaching has been sought in terms of the *ordo salutis*.[1] On the other hand, in the locus of christology or the accomplishment of redemption, dogmatic reflection has tended to concentrate almost exclusively on the sufferings and death of Christ understood as an atonement for sin. Interest in the resurrection for the most part has been restricted to its apologetic value and as a stimulus to faith. When it has received limited dogmatic attention as the initial phase of the *state of exaltation*, it has been viewed as sealing the effec-

---

1. Here and throughout this study the expression *ordo salutis* is not being used in the wider sense it has in the earlier Reformed dogmaticians; rather, as has become customary, it refers to the application of redemption in the life history of the individual sinner.

tiveness and facilitating the applicability of the redemption
wrought by Christ's death.[2]

(2) Another controlling factor is the relatively recent acceptance of a biblical-theological approach to Scripture in
Reformed circles. The explanation for this no doubt lies in
the fact that the method as initially employed was bonded to
rationalistic presuppositions which made it an inevitable and
effective instrument for the denial of the divine origin and
unity of Scripture.[3] Only gradually has orthodox scholarship

2. The statements in this paragraph are generalizations and therefore subject to
qualification and supplementation. As generalizations, however, they do have
definite weight and validity. It is true that Reformed theology has not been guilty of
the one-sided Paulinism of Lutheran theology. It has not, for instance, made the
proclamation of justification by faith a virtual criterion of canonicity. Still in fidelity
to its Reformation roots it has continued to find nothing to be more characteristic
and important to Paul than the notion of a graciously imputed righteousness. The
legitimacy of the above observations respecting christology or the accomplishment
of redemption, may be easily verified by a summary perusal of the standard works
on dogmatics. Charles Hodge, *Systematic Theology* (New York: Charles Scribner's
Sons, 1893), vol. 2, devotes four pages to the resurrection (pp. 626-630) in contrast
with a lengthy treatment of the atonement (pp. 464-591). W. G. T. Shedd, *Dogmatic
Theology* (Grand Rapids: Zondervan, n. d.), vol. 2, passes directly from a discussion
of "Vicarious Atonement" (pp. 378ff.) to "Regeneration" (pp. 490ff.). The major
writings of B. B. Warfield in this area concentrate exclusively upon the death of
Christ understood as atonement (*Biblical Doctrines* [New York: Oxford University
Press, 1929], pp. 327-445; *Studies in Theology* [New York: Oxford University Press,
1932], pp. 261-297.). The approach of Louis Berkhof, *Systematic Theology* (Grand
Rapids: Eerdmans, 1959), is similar to that of Hodge. After a brief discussion of the
resurrection (pp. 346-349) he moves on to a lengthy treatment of the atonement (pp.
361-399). The approaches of Abraham Kuyper, *Dictaten Dogmatiek*, Locus de
Christo, pars secunda (Grand Rapids: B. Sevensma, n. d.), 3: 109-114, and Herman
Bavinck, *Gereformeerde Dogmatiek*, 3: 425ff. provide no significant exceptions to this
general pattern. This virtual equation of the accomplishment of redemption with
atonement which characterizes traditional Reformed dogmatics is nowhere made
more clear or expressed more programmatically than in the opening sentence of
John Murray, *Redemption—Accomplished and Applied*: "The accomplishment of
redemption is concerned with what has been generally called the atonement" (p. 13;
cf. the opening sentence of the preface). In calling attention to this preoccupation
with the atonement, my purpose is not at all to challenge the validity and necessity
of this development, far less to call into question the conclusions reached. Rather I
wish only to point out that this dominating interest in the death of Christ has had
associated with it a relative neglect of the resurrection. Here again it is not as if
Reformed theology has had no insight into the matter. For example, Berkhof (p. 349)
writes: "What is still more important, the resurrection enters as a constitutive element
into the very essence of the work of redemption, and therefore of the gospel." But this
observation is not developed; nor is the resurrection effectively related to the structure of redemption.

3. Cf. Kuyper, *Encyclopaedie der Heilige Godgeleerdheid*, 3: 167-170, 401-405. The
sources for the rise of modern biblical theology have been conveniently collected
and edited by W. G. Kümmel, *The New Testament: The History of the Investigation of
Its Problems*, trans. S. M. Gilmour and H. C. Kee (Nashville: Abingdon, 1972), pp.
98-107; cf. the survey of O. Betz in *The Interpreter's Dictionary of the Bible* (New
York: Abingdon), 2: 432-437.

come to recognize that biblical revelation is given as an organically unfolding process, that is, as a *history*, and that therefore dealing with the biblical writers in terms of their respective places in this history, that is, with respect to their individual contributions, is not only desirable but necessary. Consequently, in the Reformed tradition of interpretation there are only two attempts to deal comprehensively with the teaching of Paul as a distinct unit. These are Geerhardus Vos's study on Pauline eschatology[4] and the recent volume of Herman Ridderbos.[5] Both these works will be referred to repeatedly below. Here our concern is with their programmatic importance.

Both men have, independently,[6] come to the same basic conclusion. Further, this conclusion represents a marked shift so far as the traditional Reformed consensus is concerned. The center of Paul's teaching is not found in the doctrine of justification by faith or any other aspect of the *ordo salutis*. Rather, his primary interest is seen to be in the *historia salutis* as that history has reached its eschatological realization in the death and especially the resurrection of Christ.

With Vos this shift is not immediately evident, although it is given with the title, *The Pauline Eschatology*. This title can be misleading to the reader who understands "eschatology" in terms of the *loci* method of dogmatics. He looks for a specialized study of the "last things" associated with the future parousia of Christ. Vos, however, intends something more. In the opening chapter he states that "to unfold the Apostle's eschatology means to set forth his theology as a whole";[7] and in this chapter he is concerned for the most part with uncovering the foundations and basic structure of Paul's thought. Chapter II is an implicit rejection of the notion that the *ordo salutis* as traditionally conceived, or a particular aspect thereof, is Paul's central interest. Rather he views the present soteriological realities of the believer's experience out of a broader eschatological perspective and as themselves the realization of the *eschaton*.

Ridderbos likewise maintains that a redemptive-historical or eschatological orientation governs Paul:

4. *The Pauline Eschatology*. (Princeton, N.J.: Princeton University Press, 1930). This work appeared originally in 1930 and has been reprinted several times.
5. *Paul. An Outline of His Theology*, trans. J. Richard DeWitt (Grand Rapids: Eerdmans, 1975). The Dutch original appeared in 1966.
6. Ridderbos is aware of Vos's work but makes only minimal reference to it.
7. *Eschatology*, p. 11; cf. p. 28.

> It is this great redemptive-historical framework within which the whole of Paul's preaching must be understood and all of its subordinate parts receive their place and organically cohere. . . . It is from this [eschatological or redemptive-historical] principal point of view and under this denominator that all the separate themes of Paul's preaching can be understood and penetrated in their unity and relation to each other.[8]

This point is stressed repeatedly.[9] Moreover, Ridderbos appears to be aware that he is making a new emphasis, at least so far as the tradition in which he stands is concerned. He deliberately employs the *heilshistorisch/heilsordelijk* distinction, which he uses in a variety of contexts to underscore that the apostle's interest is the former (i.e., redemptive-historical) rather than the latter (i.e., in terms of *ordo salutis*).[10]

In view of the dominant, indeed constitutive place Pauline material has always had in the formulations of Reformed soteriology, specifically its *ordo salutis,* there is little difficulty in sensing that far-reaching dogmatic consequences may be involved in this changed assessment of the apostle. What is particularly important for the present study is the fact that their common conclusion concerning Paul's basic outlook brings both Vos and Ridderbos to a new and deepened appreciation of the central place of Christ's *resurrection* in his teaching. According to Ridderbos, for Paul the resurrection of Jesus is the central event of redemptive history.[11] Consequently, it is the center of his preaching.[12] His eschatology (which is his theology) is pointedly "resurrection-eschatology."[13] Vos seeks to be more penetrating. He is interested in "the religious and doctrinal principles underlying the resurrection," and develops at some length the thesis that "Paul has first made it a focus of *fundamental* Christian teaching and built around it the entire conception of the faith advocated and propagated by him."[14]

This combination of factors, then—the relative neglect of Christ's resurrection by traditional Reformed dogmatics and

8. *Paul*, pp. 39, 44.
9. Cf., eg., pp. 49, 65, 162, 208, 429f., 516.
10. Pp. 14, 63, 173f., 205f., 211; cf. pp. 45f., 91, 214ff., 221f., 268f., 365, 378, 404f., and cf. H. Ridderbos, *When the Time Had Fully Come*, Pathway Books (Grand Rapids: Eerdmans, 1957), pp. 47-59.
11. *Paul*, p. 55.
12. Ibid., p. 537.
13. Ibid., p. 57.
14. *Eschatology*, pp. 147f. The italics are Vos's.

the renewed interest of recent Reformed biblical theology in what Paul has to say on the subject—defines the orbit in which we will consider the place of the resurrection in Paul's soteriology. Approaching the topic in this fashion necessitates certain restrictions. Our focal interest is in the *doctrinal* significance of the resurrection for Paul. What is its distinguishing redemptive efficacy, its specific soteric efficiency? This means that matters in themselves important such as the nature of the resurrection body, the question of the empty tomb, or the debate concerning alleged development in his teaching on resurrection will be dealt with only as they have a bearing on this central question.

In keeping with the basic conception of this study, attention will be given primarily to the Reformed interpretation of Paul, but viewpoints of other traditions will not be neglected. Even with expanded horizons, however, the available literature is decidedly limited. The primary explanation for this no doubt lies in the wider applicability of the observation already made with reference to Reformed theology. Western theology since the time of Anselm, particularly in its dogmatic reflection, has concentrated heavily, if not exclusively, upon the death of Christ. This emphasis, in turn, has governed its approach to Paul's soteriology.[15] At any rate, treatment of his views respecting the saving significance of the resurrection as a distinct theme has been restricted to several short articles appearing in various periodicals. The lengthy study of the Roman Catholic scholar, D. M. Stanley, appears to be the exception.[16] Pertinent material is, of course, to be found in commentaries, the various New Testament theologies and theologies of Paul,[17] and in some of the

---

15. Cf. M. Barth and V. H. Fletcher, *Acquittal By Resurrection* (New York: Holt, Rinehart and Winston, 1964), p. v: "Moreover, even if one adopts a broader historical perspective, it is noteworthy that, unlike the Eastern theological tradition, Western theological thought, while affirming that 'on the third day he rose again from the dead,' has nonetheless given relatively more weight to the crucifixion as the primary dimension of the Christ event."; A. M. Ramsey, *The Resurrection of Christ* (Philadelphia: The Westminster Press, 1946), pp. 117ff.; G. C. Berkouwer, *The Work of Christ*, trans. C. Lambregtse (Grand Rapids: Eerdmans, 1965), pp. 192f.

16. *Christ's Resurrection in Pauline Soteriology*, Analecta Biblica, 13, (Rome: Pontifical Biblical Institute, 1961).

17. Here again, however, the yield is not so rewarding as might be expected. Usually the death and resurrection of Christ are dealt with together with almost exclusive stress on the former. Fairly typical is the treatment of D. E. H. Whiteley, *The Theology of St. Paul* (Philadelphia: Fortress Press, 1964). In the chapter, "The Whole Work of Christ" (pp. 130-154), he devotes roughly a page to the resurrection (pp. 151f.).

longer monographs on the apostle's thought. Here again the work of Vos and Ridderbos, particularly the former, is important. It is fair to say that this study is primarily an attempt to develop and put in a somewhat broader setting the brief, but exceedingly rich and provocative sketch that Vos has given of Paul's resurrection theology.[18]

In these introductory remarks a shift in Reformed thinking concerning Paul's distinguishing interest has been tentatively established. Usually when such a turn takes place, particularly *within* a tradition, it signals a corresponding change in approach and method. Part I will attempt to show that a change in method has in fact taken place and to give some attention to the proper *way* to approach Paul. Part II will seek to uncover the basic structure of his resurrection theology and to identify the central theme which governs the whole. Part III will discuss the way Paul develops and makes use of this theme. The Conclusion will note some implications for the problems and program of Reformed dogmatics.

18. *Eschatology*, pp. 147-171.

PART ONE

Methodological Considerations

GEERHARDUS VOS'S *Pauline Eschatology* is of abiding value not only for its rich and penetrating analysis of the basic elements of Paul's teaching but also for its variety of instructive statements concerning the *way* he approaches Paul. This methodological or hermeneutical significance of the book, which so far appears to have been entirely overlooked, is that to which we now will give careful attention.

Vos's approach to Paul is controlled by his conviction that Paul can "justly be called the father of Christian eschatology" (p. vi) and even that Paul's is "the genius of the greatest constructive mind ever at work on the data of Christianity" (p. 149). Statements with a similar tone can be multiplied. Because the apostle's mind "had by nature a certain systematic bent, which made him pursue with great resoluteness the consequences of given premises" (p. 60), and because it was "highly doctrinal and synthetic" (p. 148), one must think in terms of Paul's "theological system" (p. 60), his "system of truth," his "construction of Christian truth" (p. 148). Paul's "energetic eschatological thinking tended toward consolidation in an orb of compact theological structure" (p. 61). The facile one-sidedness of which all too many of his interpreters have been guilty results in part "because Paul's mind as a theological thinker was far more exacting than theirs . . ." (p. 149).[1]

Taken together, these statements make an unmistakable impression. In particular, two factors stand out. (1) They reflect a deep appreciation of the distinctiveness and individuality of Paul, specifically his capacity as a *thinker*. The nature of Paul's mind is reflected upon in some detail. (2) They show a definite sense of continuity between Paul and

---

1. Cf. *Biblical Theology*, p. 17: "The Gospel having a precise, doctrinal structure, the doctrinally-gifted Paul was the fit organ for expressing this, because his gifts had been conferred and cultivated in advance with a view to it." (This volume, which first appeared in 1948, is a reworking of class lectures given at Princeton Theological Seminary, prior to Vos's retirement in 1932.).

his interpreter. Both have a common interest: the "data of Christianity." Christian eschatological reflection has Paul as its initiator, its "father." Moreover, the nature of this continuity, its specifically "theological" character, is indicated in a variety of ways. In short, it is not going too far to say that Vos approaches the apostle as one with whom he is involved in a common theological enterprise. And he does this without any sense of incompatibility with a conviction of the unity and divine origin and authority of Scripture.

Vos's approach stands in sharp contrast to Abraham Kuyper's rejection of the expression "biblical theology."[2] This contrast is instructive because the latter's work on theological encyclopaedia has had a decisive influence in shaping Reformed theological method, an influence which continues, at least indirectly, to the present.

At a first glance Kuyper's objections appear to be primarily historical in character, based on reaction to rationalistic theology which masqueraded its thinly-veiled attacks on the authority of Scripture under the slogan, "biblical theology." This factor certainly is important,[3] but closer examination shows that his rejection has a much deeper basis.

Nothing less than the way in which Kuyper understands Scripture as the *principium theologiae* prohibits his use of the expression "biblical theology." Scripture itself is not theology but underlies it.[4] The biblical writers must not be called theologians (p. 176), because theology is unthinkable apart from previously formed dogmas, and dogma is a product of the life of the (institutional) church.[5] Thus stress is placed exclusively upon the disjunction, the discontinuity in principle, between Scripture and the biblical writers on the one hand, and the dogmas and theologians of the church on the other. The Bible itself contains no dogmas but rather the "material" out of which the church "constructs" dogma.[6] The biblical revelation is given in the "stylized, symbolic-aesthetic language of the East;" only when the "Western

2. *Encyclopaedie der Heilige Godgeleerdheid*, 3: 166-180.

3. Ibid., pp. 169f., pp. 401-404.

4. Ibid., p. 167: "If Holy Scripture is the principium of theology, then theology only *begins* when Holy Scripture is there" (Kuyper's italics).

5. Ibid., p. 169: "Dogmatics is unthinkable unless dogma has previously formed, and dogma is as such a fruit of the life-process of the *church*" (Kuyper's italics); cf. pp. 395ff.

6. Ibid.: "There are no dogmas in Holy Scripture, only the material from which the church, under the guidance of the Holy Spirit, has to construct dogmas"; p. 404: ". . . and Scripture does not provide us with dogmas themselves, but with the material from which the church has to build dogmas"; cf. pp. 355ff.

mind" with its penchant for "dialectical clarity" goes to work on the biblical material does theology come into being.[7]

It is essential to see, then, that in terms of the sequence: Scripture, church, dogma, dogmatics (theology),[8] and because of the way the stress on discontinuity is distributed, Kuyper rejects biblical theology not only in name but in *concept*. To be sure, he does go on to approve the material interest of biblical theology, namely, its concern with the historical character of the Bible. He laments the shortcomings of the *loca probantia* method of dogmatics in this respect, and looks for real progress in biblical understanding to result from a study of the *historia revelationis*.[9]

Even from these brief sketches it is not difficult to recognize a decided difference in emphasis and approach between Vos and Kuyper. In fact, the stress of the one is precisely the opposite of the other. (1) Kuyper's construction is characterized by a "leveling" treatment of the biblical authors. In the sphere of *encyclopaedia* no attempt is made to take into account their respective differences. In fact, it seems there is an implicit tendency in the opposite direction.[10] While Vos thinks in terms of the "systematic bent" and the "highly doctrinal and synthetic" quality of Paul's mind,[11] for Kuyper, the apostle, along with the other biblical writers, speaks the "stylized, symbolic-aesthetic language of the East."[12] (2) Kuyper stresses exclusively the *discontinuity*

---

7. Ibid., p. 168: "Revelation is given to us in Holy Scripture, wrapped in the symbolic-aesthetic language of the East. Its content is now transferred out of the oriental world into that western consciousness which attempts to bring the general human consciousness to dialectical clarity; and only where this transition takes place does theology originate"; cf. vol. II, pp. 247f.

8. Just how determinative and clearly defined this pattern of distinctions is in Kuyper's thinking appears from the fact that it furnishes the designations for three of the four major subdivisions of special encyclopaedia: De Bibliologische, De Ecclesiologische and De Dogmatologische (which includes dogmatics).

9. *Encyclopaedie*, 3: 170ff.

10. Ibid., p. 176: "Certainly each one of these men lived in a religious thought-world, and this thought-world is used in revelation, used even with the individual variations which more than one of them discloses; but in the history of revelation both this religious thought-world and these individual variations do service only as the canvas on which the Holy Spirit embroiders; and not that canvas but the embroidery itself is that which constitutes revelation and with which we should be concerned."

11. Cf. *Biblical Theology*, p. 16: "The didactic, dialectic mentality of Paul. . . ."

12. It is difficult to see how anyone who has read the letters of Paul could make such a generalization. Apparently Kuyper's encyclopaedic interests have at this point blinded him to what he himself recognizes elsewhere: "What makes the letters of Paul so difficult is that there the mystical-oriental and western-dialectical streams flow into each other" (*Dictaten Dogmatiek*, vol. I, part 2, p. 54); "Paul is a more acute thinker than James . . ." (*Encyclopaedie*, 2: 241).

between the biblical writers and the theological activity of subsequent Christian generations. Accordingly, Vos's description of Paul as a specifically "theological" thinker and his repeated references to the apostle's "theological system" are modes of expression forbidden to Kuyper *in principle.*

These two points of view are mutually exclusive in key respects. Which, if either, is correct? Kuyper's position may represent the characteristically Reformed attitude, particularly concerning the relationship between the interpretation of Paul and dogmatic formulation. Nevertheless, a variety of considerations points to Vos's approach as the proper way to deal with Paul as a biblical writer, that is, as an instrument of revelation.[13]

Biblical revelation has an *historical* interest. Scripture is a record of the history of revelation, which includes its own production. Analysis of this history—analysis welcomed by Kuyper himself—has made increasingly clear that revelation is a differentiated phenomenon, coming as acts or words. God reveals himself both in redemption and in revelation, in what he does as well as in what he says. The organic relationship between these two facets has also become more and more evident. Revelation never stands by itself, but is always concerned either explicitly or implicitly with redemptive accomplishment. God's speech is invariably related to his actions. It is not going too far to say that redemption is the *raison d'être* of revelation.[14] An unbiblical, quasi-gnostic notion of revelation inevitably results when it is considered by itself or as providing self-evident general truths.[15] Consequently, revelation is either authentication or interpretation of God's redemptive action. Usually both description and explanation can be found in a given biblical writer or instrument of revelation, although in each instance one element will be more prominent than the other.[16]

13. In discussing these here, attention for the most part will have to be limited to initiating and sketching lines of argument without fully expanding upon them. Many related questions, in themselves important, must be bypassed completely.
14. Vos's is still among the best discussions of this and related points (*Biblical Theology*, pp. 14f., 24, 124, 324ff.).
15. Ibid., p. 24: "Revelation is so interwoven with redemption that, unless allowed to consider the latter, it would be suspended in the air."
16. The basic structure of the New Testament canon reflects this distinction: gospels (attestation)/epistles (interpretation). That this pattern is *intentional* or *constitutive* is confirmed by the shape of Marcion's canon: edited Gospel of Luke/the Epistles of Paul with the exception of the pastorals. (For a brief presentation of the evidence favoring the position that Marcion's canon is molded according to the church's and not vice versa, cf. T. Zahn, *Grundriss der Geschichte des neutestamentlichen*

In the case of Paul, there is no doubt that the aspect of interpretation is more characteristic. The almost exclusive concern of his writing and preaching is expounding, "exegeting" the history of redemption as it has reached its climax in the death and resurrection of Christ. In Paul's perspective, Christ's place in the history of revelation is conditioned by and exponential of a specific redemptive-historical context. This is a decisively important perspective for understanding Paul. Only as it is appreciated together with its implications does the real significance of his revelatory functions become apparent.

One of these implications especially concerns us at this point. From the perspective of the history of redemption believers today are in the same situation as was Paul.[17] Together with him they look back upon the climactic events of Christ's death, resurrection, and ascension, while together with him they "wait for his Son from heaven" (I Thess. 1:10), the one event in that history which is still outstanding. The same tension between "already" and "not yet" which marked Paul's experience characterizes the life of the believer today.

Thus the continuity between Paul and his interpreters is clear. Specifically, they are related in terms of a common redemptive-historical index. Moreover, in view of the correlation between redemptive act and revelatory word, that is, Scripture's own focus on the history of redemption, the pointedly *theological* nature of this continuity is also apparent. This follows on the assumption that theology ought to be based on the text of Scripture, that as an historical discipline biblical exegesis is likewise theologically normative. Thus if Paul's interest is interpreting the history of redemption, then

Kanons (Leipzig: A. Deichert, 1904), pp. 28f. The recent recovery of the *Gospel of Truth* in extant form strengthens this position.) As indicated above, the distinction between attestation and interpretation may not be applied in a rigid fashion, as if the Gospels contain no interpretation and the Epistles no authentication. Such a construction would obviously fail to do justice to the teaching of Jesus. Still, the fundamental perspective from which the New Testament is an organic whole (i.e., canon) is that Jesus (including his teaching) and the apostles (particularly their letters) are related as "the great fact to be expounded" and "the subsequent interpretation of this fact" (Vos, *Biblical Theology*, pp. 324f.).

17. *Ibid.*, p. 325f.: "Still we know full well that we ourselves live just as much in the New Testament as did Peter and Paul and John." In the same context Vos makes the perceptive and highly suggestive observation that the seeming disproportion between the chronological extent of the Old Testament and that of the New Testament "arises from viewing the new revelation too much by itself, and not sufficiently as *introductory* and *basic* to the large period following" (p. 325, my italics).

the interpretation of Paul necessarily has the same interest, carried out in a common redemptive-historical context. Theology, whatever may be its scope and final shape, can have no more basic interest than to follow in Paul's footsteps by explaining and interpreting the redemptive-historical tension which characterizes the believer's existence, by expounding and elucidating "the mystery which has been kept secret for long ages past, but now is manifested . . ." (Rom. 16:25f.). In a word, the concept of theology is redemptive-historically conditioned. The essence of theology is interpretation of the history of redemption. Consequently, a theological continuity necessarily exists between Paul and his interpreters.

Biblical theology is generally viewed as a survey of the progression of the redemptive-revelatory activity of God in history, carried out from a later and basically (i.e., redemptive-historically) different vantage point. This, most properly, is a description of Old Testament biblical theology. To be sure, concern with the progress of revelation is not lacking in New Testament biblical theology, but what distinguishes it is the fact that, in the manner noted above, the exegete, despite every cultural and temporal dissimilarity, stands in principle (i.e., in terms of the history of redemption) in the same situation as the writers of the New Testament and, therefore, is involved with Paul (and the other letter writers) in a common interpretative enterprise.[18]

This line of thought may be put somewhat differently by observing that Paul's function in the economy of revelation cannot be divorced from his office and functioning as apostle. In other words, his activity as an instrument of revelation is qualified *ecclesiastically*. This, in turn, means that the inspired, infallible revelation given through him is at the same time the authoritative teaching and opinion (= dogma) of the church, and that, as various dogmas display obvious relationships to each other, one may speak of his theology.

At least some of the methodological considerations already introduced have relevance for the study of the entire New Testament, particularly the Epistles. Here, however, their

18. This difference in program between Old Testament biblical theology and New Testament biblical theology is already intimated by B. B. Warfield, "The Person of Christ," *Biblical Doctrines* (New York: Oxford University Press, 1929), p. 176: "In its fundamental teaching, the New Testament lends itself, therefore, more readily to what is called dogmatic than to what is called genetic treatment. . . ." This observation is especially germane to the writings of Paul.

applicability for Pauline studies needs to be stressed. They provide the perspective for properly viewing his writings in their distinctiveness. Specifically, the pervasively didactic or doctrinal nature of Paul's teaching ought to be approached while recognizing common redemptive-historical interest and common redemptive-historical situation. The at times closely-reasoned character of Paul's letters hardly needs to be argued, particularly where Reformed scholarship is concerned.[19] But an awareness of the redemptive-historical factors involved is necessary to appreciate the deeper significance of this doctrinal quality and systematic interest. This awareness provides the warrant for speaking of Paul's theology in the proper sense of the word. At least with respect to Paul, then, it is in order to say that the *principium theologiae*, Scripture, itself contains theology or, perhaps better, that the nature of the continuity between our theology and its *principium* (the Bible) is at points distinctly *theological*. Kuyper's sequence, therefore, is at least subject to supplementation. Recognition of the discontinuity between the New Testament and its subsequent interpretation in the church needs to be balanced by recognizing the (ecclesiastical-theological, redemptive-historical) continuity between them.[20]

So far our discussion has tried to vindicate and develop Geerhardus Vos's approach to Paul by showing (1) that Paul's interpreters ought to deal with him as they stand with him in the same redemptive-historical context and so share a common interpretative interest, and (2) that in this light they are

19. Cf., e.g., Warfield (*Biblical Doctrines*, p. 176), who refers to Paul as "the most didactic of the New Testament writers." One may assume that even Kuyper would not take exception to this statement.

20. There is no need to read out of the argument developed to this point any unbiblical qualification or relativizing of the perfections of Scripture (necessity, authority, clarity, sufficiency!). An analogy from differential calculus may help to make the basic points clear. Redemptive events constitute a function (f), the authentication and interpretation of the New Testament its first derivative (f′) and the interpretation of the later church its second derivative (f″). F′, to be sure, is of a different order than f″, since the former, the infallible verbal revelation (Scripture) which has God as its primary author, is the basis (*principium*) of the latter. But both, as derivatives, have a common *interpretative* reference to f. Indeed, it may be said that at its level (characterized by fallibility and tentativeness) f″ "goes beyond" f′ by seeking to make more explicit the structure implicit in the latter.

In the above discussion, the redemptive-historical distinction between canonical and noncanonical, between the apostolic and postapostolic periods, is *not* being overlooked or obliterated. Rather, stress has been placed on some implications of the fact that in "church" the "apostolic" and "postapostolic" have their common (redemptive-historical) denominator.

to do justice to his doctrinal interest, his distinctiveness as a thinker. This stress on continuity may be expressed by viewing Paul as a *theologian*. This fundamental point of departure gives rise to several conclusions essential to a comprehensive understanding of his teaching.

(1) To approach Paul as a theologian means that no encyclopaedic structure or set of distinctions may be allowed to make the situation in which he developed the teaching of his Epistles incommensurable in principle with the various contexts in which the later church has hammered out her doctrines. In terms of the history of redemption, for instance, the structure of Paul's soteriological teaching may be contrasted and compared directly with the structure of Reformed soteriology. In other words, to state the broader methodological implication, biblical theology and systematic theology may not be arbitrarily and artificially separated. The proper interest of the former is revelation as an *historical process.* Inevitably, then, it draws attention to the distinguishing characteristics and peculiarities of what the respective biblical authors have written. The significant gain, however, is not that the "humanness" of the Bible is thereby underscored. In and of itself this is of no value. Rather, because attention is on the human instrumentality in giving revelation, God's activity is made more specific and so the *structure* of that revelation as *product,* the proper concern of dogmatics, comes into sharper focus.[21]

21. In view of this consideration, an "incursion" of biblical theology (concern with revelation *qua* process) into the domain of systematic theology (concern with revelation *qua* product) is both inevitable and necessary. In need of at least qualification is the customary Reformed attempt to distinguish the two disciplines with respect to *method.* Cf. J. Murray, "Systematic Theology. Second Article," *WTJ,* 26 (1963-64):33: "The difference is merely one of method. Biblical theology deals with the data of special revelation from the standpoint of its history; systematic theology deals with the same in its totality as a finished product."; Vos, *Biblical Theology,* p. 13: "Biblical Theology deals with revelation as a divine activity, not as the finished product of that activity." However, Murray, toward the end of the article just quoted, makes the following important observation: "But systematic theology will fail of its task to the extent to which it discards its rootage in biblical theology as properly conceived and developed. It might seem that an undue limitation is placed upon systematic theology by requiring that the exegesis with which it is so intimately concerned should be regulated by the principle of biblical theology. And it might seem contrary to the canon so important to both exegesis and systematics, namely, the analogy of Scripture. These appearances do not correspond to reality. The fact is that only when systematic theology is rooted in biblical theology does it exemplify its true function and achieve its purposes" (pp. 45f.). For a fuller discussion of this relationship, see my "Systematic Theology and Biblical Theology," *WTJ,* 38, 3 (Spring 1976): 281-299.

This mutual interest of biblical theology and systematic theology is especially prominent in the study of Paul. If as a theologian his letters and preaching disclose a structure of thought, then it follows that the shape an exegetically-based theology takes should reflect that structure as explicitly as possible,[22] especially in the locus of soteriology where Pauline material inevitably figures so prominently. If, in the common activity of theologizing, Paul, as apostle and instrument of revelation, is distinguished from his interpreters by providing part of the inspired and indispensable foundation (the *principium*) for subsequent theological activity, it follows that his interpreters should be concerned not only with the material, the particular conceptions found in Paul, but also with the *way* in which Paul himself handles this material and structures the various conceptions.

As long as one continues with Kuyper to speak of the Bible as providing the "material" out of which the church "constructs" dogmas and develops a dogmatics, it is difficult to see how the *loca probantia* method is really and effectively overcome, despite insistence to the contrary. As long as one operates with his encyclopaedic distinctions, the synthesizing principles employed by Paul will at best be only obscurely perceived and so, almost inevitably, replaced either implicitly or explicitly by others foreign to him. Scripture must determine not only the content but also the *method* of theology.[23]

(2) To approach Paul as a theologian helps to define the *problem* of Pauline interpretation. From the very beginning the church has had its difficulties with Paul's writings, as Peter himself verifies. He acknowledges that they contain "some things which are hard to understand" and alludes to the disastrous consequences resulting from their misuse in certain quarters (II Peter 3:16). This statement not only attests the antiquity of the problem of Pauline interpretation; it also gives to that problem, one may say, *canonical* proportions.

---

22. Cf. M. Kline, *By Oath Consigned* (Grand Rapids: Eerdmans, 1968), p. 29: "Surely it does not become systematic theology to unravel what has been synthesized to a degree even in the Scriptures. Systematic theology ought rather to weave together the related strands yet more systematically."

23. Cf. P. Lengsfeld, *Adam und Christus*, Koinonia—Beiträge zur ökumenischen Spiritualität und Theologie, 9, ed. T. Sartory (Essen: Ludgerus-Verlag, 1965), p. 22: "Scripture is also canon for the task of dogmatics (not only for its content)."

The history of Pauline interpretation has been characterized by an excess of ingenuity and a dearth of real penetra-
tion. Interpretation has tended to take exploratory outings
when it should have been digging deeper. Only too seldom
has it gone deep enough.[24] However, it is not only the
variety of defects on the interpreters' side which has so often
barred the way to a deepened understanding of Paul. Rather,
involved here as well is the "proper" problem of Pauline interpretation.

The real difficulty for interpretation lies in the fact that in
Paul's writings we encounter a thinker of constructive
genius, with a dogmatic bent, but only as he directs himself
to specific situations and questions, only as he expresses himself in "occasional" fashion. In short, the true problem in understanding Paul is that he is a theologian, a careful and
systematic thinker, accessible only through pastoral letters
and records of his sermons. His writings are obviously not
doctrinal treatises; but neither do they consist in a variety of
unrelated, *ad hoc* formulations or in an unsystematic mul-
tiplication of conceptions. They reflect a structure of thought.
The Pauline epistles may be aptly compared to the visible
portion of an iceberg. What juts above the surface is but a
small fraction of what remains submerged. The true
proportions of the whole lie hidden beneath the surface.[25]
The contours of what can be seen at a first glance may also
prove deceptive. Put less pictorially, that conception or line
of thought having relatively little explicit textual support, on
reflection may prove to be of the most basic, constitutive
significance. This state of affairs makes the interpretation of
Paul, particularly a comprehensive attempt, an inherently
difficult and precarious undertaking.

(3) Consequently, to approach Paul as a theologian helps
to pinpoint the fundamental *task* of Pauline interpretation.
Here we can hardly do better than formulate with Vos. "Our
task consists of ascertaining the perspective of thought in the

---

24. Albert Schweitzer's verdict on nineteenth century "historical-critical" study of
Paul has a wider range of application in this respect: "The study of Paulinism has
nothing very brilliant to show for itself in the way of scientific achievement. Learn-
ing has been lavishly expended upon it, but thought and reflection have been to
seek" (*Paul and His Interpreters*, trans. W. Montgomery [London: Adam and Charles
Black, 1912], p. 237).

25. Cf. Warfield, *Biblical Doctrines*, p. 175, where he speaks of the conception of
Christ's person "which lies on—or, if we prefer to say so, beneath—the pages of the
New Testament."

revealed Gospel delivered by the Apostle. . . . It is the subtle weaving of these threads of perspective into the doctrinal fabric of thought as a whole that we must endeavor, so far as possible, to unravel."[26] The interpretation of Paul above all involves careful attention to underlying structure. In his writings and preaching we encounter a mind of unusual constructive energy with an unparalleled capacity for synthetic thinking, in a word (again with Vos), a "master-mind."[27] Interpretation which fails to reckon with this fact obscures both the breadth and the depth of his teaching. With a sense of redemptive history, with an understanding of himself as one, together with Paul, "upon whom the ends of the ages have come" (I Cor. 10:11), the interpreter ought to be intent on articulating the structure of thought reflected in his statements, on an ever-clearer refraction of what Vos has described as that "luminosity radiating from the core of condensed ideas."[28]

(4) Finally, to speak of Paul as a theologian means pointedly that his governing interest lies in explicating the history of redemption. This conclusion, based on general observations respecting the place of Paul's letters within the structure of biblical revelation, already decides the issue raised in the introduction. *How* this concern of Paul with the *historia salutis* also provides for an *ordo salutis* is a separate question, one which can only be answered by a careful examination of the text. However, it may be maintained here as a working principle, subject to further verification, that whatever treatment Paul gives to the application of salvation to the individual believer is controlled by his redemptive-historical outlook.

* * *

Reflections on method are inevitably related to the area of investigation. They presuppose (and require) a high degree

---

26. *Eschatology*, p. 44.
27. Ibid., p. vi. Without approving his conception of Paul's mysticism, well worth repeating in this connection is the statement of Schweitzer, *The Mysticism of Paul the Apostle*, trans. W. Montgomery (New York: Henry Holt, 1931), p. 139: "And how totally wrong those are who refuse to admit that Paul was a logical thinker, and proclaim as the highest outcome of their wisdom the discovery that he has no system! For he is a logical thinker and his mysticism is a complete system." Cf. E. Käsemann, *New Testament Questions of Today*, trans. W. J. Montague (Philadelphia: Fortress Press, 1969), p. 177: "But Paul's theology is always carefully thought out: the last adjective one could apply to it would be 'naive.' "
28. *Eschatology*, p. 302.

of acquaintance with the subject matter to be studied. Similarly, only the concrete act of application discloses their relative validity and appropriateness. This is uniquely so with the interpretation of Scripture, because the text by virtue of its divine origin is self-interpreting. In particular, the last of the conclusions drawn above suggests that our discussion on method has come full circle, at least so far as the present study is concerned. Accordingly, we turn now to a consideration of the place of Christ's resurrection in Paul's soteriology. A continually underlying and accompanying interest will be the legitimacy and fruitfulness of the approach indicated in this chapter.

PART TWO

---

*THE RESURRECTION OF
CHRIST IN PAUL'S
SOTERIOLOGY:*

The Central Theme and
Basic Structure

A SPECIAL DIFFICULTY besets the interpretation of Paul. His writings and preaching clearly provide a coherent body of teaching. Yet the bonds of this cohesiveness frequently lie beneath the surface of the text. As a result, the interpreter may sense relationships between elements of teaching without grasping just *how* they are related or the priority of each relative to the others. To the extent that this lack of structural insight persists, an improper linking of conceptions is inevitable. The result, in turn, will be either a more or less arbitrary imposition of a structure foreign to the material or a sense of confusion, made all the more baffling and disconcerting simply because one has become entangled in lines of interdependence which are so real.

This problem becomes especially compounded with a matter so basic as the resurrection of Jesus. Here the interweaving of ideas is so varied and complex that the apostle's perspective is particularly subject to distortion. In other words, here the interpreter must be especially sensitive to *structure*. Consequently, it is essential to begin by showing that running through the relevant material is a central theme which governs the whole: the unity of the resurrection of Christ and the resurrection of believers. Such an approach may initially seem a bit contrived, but its validity and value will become increasingly apparent as the discussion develops.

THE RESURRECTION OF CHRIST AND THE
FUTURE RESURRECTION OF BELIEVERS

The fact of union or solidarity between Christ and believers in the experience of bodily resurrection is on the surface of the text at several points and in these instances need not be argued at length.

I Corinthians 15:20ff.

The notion of unity is expressed most clearly and graphically in I Corinthians 15:20, where Christ by virtue of his resurrection is described as "the firstfruits of those who are asleep" (cf. v. 23). The word "firstfruits" ($\dot{\alpha}\pi\alpha\rho\chi\dot{\eta}$) in this expression is our particular concern. As Johannes Weiss has put it: "This little word contains a thesis."[1] There can be little question that the Septuagint provides the background for its use here.[2] There, with few exceptions, "firstfruits" has a specifically cultic significance. It refers to the "firstfruits" offerings of grain, wine, cattle, and the like, appointed by Moses.[3] The point to these sacrifices is that they are not offered up for their own sake, as it were, but as representative of the total harvest, the entire flock, and so forth. They are a token expression of recognition and thanksgiving that the whole has been given by God.[4] Thus "firstfruits" does not simply have a temporal force. It does bring into view the initial portion of the harvest, but only as it is part of the whole; it focuses on the first of the newborn lambs only as they belong to the entire flock. "Firstfruits" expresses the notion of organic connection and unity, the inseparability of the initial quantity from the whole. It is particularly this aspect which gives these sacrifices their significance.

These ideas of representation and organic unity—apart from the specifically cultic connotations of the Septuagint usage—find expression in the use of "firstfruits" in I Corinthians 15:20. The word is not simply an indication of temporal priority.[5] Rather it brings into view Christ's resurrection as the "firstfruits" of the resurrection-harvest, the initial portion of the whole. His resurrection is the representative beginning of the resurrection of believers. In other words, the term seems deliberately chosen to make evident

---

1. *Der erste Korintherbrief*, MeyerK, 5, 10th ed. (Göttingen: Vandenhoeck & Ruprecht, 1925), p. 356.
2. The papyri give little illumination. "It is clear that the connotation 'first-fruits' could not be pressed in our exegesis of the term when it appears in the NT, apart from associations wholly outside the field surveyed in this article . . ." (J. H. Moulton and G. Milligan, *The Vocabulary of the Greek New Testament Illustrated from the Papyri and Other Non-Literary Sources* [London: Hodder and Stoughton, 1930], p. 54).
3. E.g., Exod. 23:19; Lev. 23:10; Num. 15:20f.; 18:8, 11f.; Deut. 18:4; 26:2, 10.
4. This token-aspect is made especially clear in Deut. 26:1f., 10; cf. Lev. 23:10; Num. 18:30.
5. Against G. Delling, *TDNT*, 1:486.

the organic connection between the two resurrections. In the context, Paul's "thesis" over against his opponents[6] is that the resurrection of Jesus has the bodily resurrection of "those who sleep"[7] as its necessary consequence. His resurrection is not simply a guarantee; it is a pledge in the sense that it is the actual beginning of the general event. In fact, on the basis of this verse it can be said that Paul views the two resurrections not so much as two events but as two episodes of the same event.[8] At the same time, however, he clearly maintains a temporal distinction between them. "Then" (v. 23) makes this apparent.

The occurrences of "firstfruits" elsewhere in Paul all express the notion of organic connection. In the parallel construction of Romans 11:16, the first clause reasons from the "firstfruits" (of dough) to the whole lump, the second clause from the root to the branches. Since the relation between the first portion of dough and the root is not exactly analogous (the latter unlike the former is productive), yet each is made the basis for postulation, then the specific point of the parallel and so the consideration governing the argument must be the factor of organic union. Similarly, in Romans 16:5 where Epaenetus is called "the firstfruits of Asia in Christ," the thought is not simply that he is the first convert in Ephesus. Rather he stands out in Paul's mind as the beginning of the manifold yield produced by the preaching of the gospel (cf. I Cor. 16:15).[9] The broader significance of "the firstfruits of the Spirit" in Romans 8:23 will occupy us below. For the present, however, we can note that, regardless whether the genitive is partitive or appositional, the thought is plainly that the Spirit presently possessed by believers is a token, an initial enjoyment of the adoption (cf. v. 15) which hereafter will be fully and openly received in the resurrection of the body.

6. The position of the Corinthian opposition need not be pinpointed here. Whether it involved an outright denial or a "spiritualization" of the believers' resurrection, it is evident that the future, somatic aspect was repudiated.

7. This and similar expressions have reference to dead believers only (cf. v. 18 and below, p. 62, n. 86).

8. This is a conclusion drawn from this verse along a broad interpretative front. Vos (*Eschatology*, p. 45) comments in passing on the verse: "Nor is it necessary to show that Paul regards the resurrection of Jesus as the actual beginning of the general epochal event." Cf. Ridderbos, *Paul*, p. 538: "His resurrection and that of his people form an unbreakable unity."; Hermann, *Kyrios und Pneuma*, p. 115; Schweitzer, *The Mysticism of Paul*, p. 98; Bultmann, *Theology*, 1:347f.

9. Cf. Ridderbos, *Aan de Romeinen*, p. 344.

Returning now to I Corinthians 15:20, the verses immediately following strengthen our interpretation of "firstfruits." The syntactical ties between them are especially instructive. Verse 21 gives the reason for what has been said in verse 20. This is the force of "for since" (ἐπειδὴ γάρ). Verse 22, in turn, grounds the statement of verse 21. This is the force of "for" (γάρ).[10] In other words, the resurrection of the dead through man (v. 21b) and the making alive of all in Christ (v. 22b) explain the significance of Christ as "firstfruits" (v. 20). Further, verse 22 clearly expresses the idea of solidarity by contrasting Christ with Adam (cf. vv. 45, 47-49); this is a virtual one-sentence summary of the teaching in Romans 5:12ff. where the notions of solidaric relationship play such a dominant role. Hence verse 22b in particular confirms that the ideas of solidarity and organic connection are present in verse 20. Christ is "the firstfruits of those who sleep" because he is raised as the second Adam. At the same time, however, verse 22b does go beyond the idea expressed by "firstfruits" by bringing into view Christ's determinative place in this relationship: it is only as they are "in Christ," united with the second Adam,[11] that "all shall be raised."

Colossians 1:18

,Colossians 1:15ff. continues to puzzle interpreters.[12] Its difficulties, however, need concern us only as they bear on understanding the description of Christ as "firstborn from the dead" (v. 18). Like "firstfruits," the background for this use of "firstborn" (πρωτότοκος) is in the Septuagint. Moreover, there these two forms display a decided affinity. On two occasions they occur together as virtual synonyms to describe the "firstfruits" offerings (Neh. 10:36f.; Ezek. 44:30). A related term, πρωτογέννημα, is used alongside "firstfruits" several times, again synonymously to express the idea of "firstfruits" or first offspring.[13] On the basis of this usage, then, it might seem warranted to see a close connection between the ideas in I Corinthians 15:20 and Colossians 1:18. In the latter passage

---

10. Cf. F. W. Grosheide, *Commentary on the First Epistle to the Corinthians*, NICNT (Grand Rapids: Eerdmans, 1960), p. 363.

11. Cf. "those who belong to Christ" (οἱ τοῦ Χριστοῦ, v. 23; cf. v. 18).

12. The situation has been made even more complicated by the recent attempt to show that a hymn underlies these verses which is not only pre-Pauline but pre-Christian, gnostic in origin; cf., e.g., E. Käsemann, "Eine urchristliche Taufliturgie," *Exegetische Versuche und Besinnungen* (Göttingen: Vandenhoeck & Ruprecht, 1967), 1:34-51.

13. Exod. 23:16, 19; Lev. 2:14; 23:17, 20; Num. 18:12f.

the thought would be that the resurrection is analogous to the process of birth, so that, of the group which experiences resurrection-birth, Christ is "firstborn." This interpretation could find support elsewhere in Paul (Rom. 1:4; perhaps Acts 13:33).

However, other considerations point to a somewhat different understanding of this expression. Chief among these is the use of "firstborn" in verse 15. Here Christ is called "firstborn of all creation." Two qualifications bound the interpretation of this phrase, no matter how it is to be understood exactly. On the one hand, "firstborn" brings into view a relationship of Christ to creation. The term cannot express an identity or status apart from creation. On the other hand, the thought cannot be that Christ is the first creature. For this is flatly contradicted by what immediately follows. Christ is "firstborn" of all creation precisely *because* all things were created in him (v. 16).

Keeping these boundaries in view, "firstborn" is to be understood in terms of a strand of usage present in the Old Testament, where the literal force of both "first" and "born" has receded, and the term has become an indication of uniqueness, special status and dignity, marking one as the recipient of exceptional favor and blessing.[14] This usage is clearest in Exodus 4:22 where the Lord directs Moses to tell Pharoah that Israel as a nation is his (the Lord's) "firstborn," and again in Psalm 88(89):27 where he says that he will make David "firstborn, higher than the kings of the earth." This force fits the immediate context with its emphasis on the creative activity of Christ and his exaltedness over the whole creation. It also fits the general purpose of the letter to stress the uniqueness and supremacy of Christ both in redemption and creation.[15]

---

14. Cf. for the discussion immediately following, F. W. Grosheide and H. Ridderbos, *De Brief van Paulus aan de Efeziërs, Aan de Kolossenzen*, CNT (Kampen: J. H. Kok, 1960), p. 137; A. König, "Christus as Die 'Eersgeborene,' " *Ned. Geref. Teologiese Tydskrif*, 9 (1967): 83-85, 89-91.

15. This stress is at least in part directed against what appears to be a Jewish-gnostic reverence of angelic beings which obscured the uniqueness and all-sufficiency of Christ's person and work; cf. E. K. Simpson and F. F. Bruce, *Commentary on the Epistles to the Ephesians and the Colossians*, NICNT (Grand Rapids: Eerdmans, 1957), pp. 165-169; G. Bornkamm, "Die Häresie des Kolosserbriefes," *Das Ende des Gesetzes*, Gesammelte Aufsätze, 1 (München: Chr. Kaiser, 1958), pp. 139-156; D. Guthrie, *New Testament Introduction*, 3rd ed. (Downers Grove, Ill.: Inter-Varsity Press, 1970), pp. 546-550.

Apparently, then, "firstborn" in verse 18 should be understood in the light of its use in verse 15, not only because
both are in close proximity and have a common reference to
Christ, but also in view of the parallel structure of the
passage where "firstborn of all creation" corresponds to "firstborn from the dead." The primary thought in verse 18, then,
is the supremacy and authority of Christ over the dead (who
will be raised; cf. Rom. 14:8f.).[16]

However, the difference between the two expressions as
well as their parallelism must be appreciated. Specifically,
the preposition "from" (ἐκ) in verse 18 gives an indication of
what is not found in verse 15—identification and solidarity.
Only as he himself is one "from the dead" is Christ "firstborn." Only as he is part of that group which is (to be) raised
does he enjoy this exalted status.[17] Accordingly, we meet
with the same controlling thought found in the idea of Christ
as "firstfruits."[18]

The correlative expressions in verse 18 both confirm this
understanding of "firstborn" and deepen its central thrust.
"The beginning" (ἀρχή), which immediately precedes, is
likewise more than an indication of simply temporal priority.
It has a stronger force; denoting headship and primacy.[19] Especially in combination with "firstborn" it expresses pointedly the significance of Christ's resurrection: his is the
beginning of the "general epochal event" which at the same
time makes him head over the others; with his resurrection is
given the resurrection of believers.[20] Consequently, in the

---

16. Cf. W. Michaelis, *TDNT*, 6:878: ". . . a reference to the superior rank and
dignity of Christ. . . ."
17. An indication of temporal priority is also present.
18. Cf. Michaelis, *TDNT*, 6:877f.: "Nevertheless, priority in time is not the only
important aspect; included, too, is the significance which the resurrection of Christ
has as the prelude to the general resurrection at the Last Day." Cf. König, "Eersgeborene," p. 90. The notion of solidarity is also present in the only other use of
"firstborn" in Paul (Rom. 8:29: "firstborn among many brothers"). However, here
again this is so not because of the verbal adjective (which is to be understood by
analogy with its usage in Col. 1:15, 18) but by virtue of the preposition and the notion of brotherhood.
19. This force is especially clear in the instances of Septuagint usage where ἀρχή
and πρωτότοκος occur together: Gen. 49:3; Deut. 21:17; cf. E. Lohmeyer, *Die Briefe
an die Philipper, an die Kolosser und an Philemon*, MeyerK, 9, 9th ed. (Göttingen:
Vandenhoeck & Ruprecht, 1953), p. 63.
20. "We shall have to understand both qualifications in close relationship with each
other, and must thus see in 'the Beginning' a denotation of the significance of
Christ's resurrection as well. Our word 'beginning' is no adequate translation for it.
For what is intended is not merely that Christ was the First or formed a beginning
in terms of chronological order; he was rather the Pioneer, the Inaugurator, who

purpose clause which follows, the *hapax legomenon* πρωτεύων, which means literally "to be first," "to have first place," hardly has a purely temporal reference. Again, whether or not the terminology of gnostic opposition is employed here,[21] the fuller notion of preeminence and special station is present.[22] Finally, the ecclesiological and perhaps even the cosmic perspectives governing Paul's thought here should be recognized. That Christ as resurrected is "the beginning," "firstborn from the dead" and "preeminent in all" is tied in (at least syntactically) with his identity as "the head of the body, the church." Even if "head" and "body" in this and similar expressions (cf. Eph. 1:22f.; 4:15f.; 5:23) do not form a single physiological metaphor but combine two figures, the former having reference to Christ's cosmic supremacy,[23] the notions of representation and organic connection are still integrally present.[24]

Conclusion. Colossians 1:18, particularly in designating Christ "firstborn from the dead," contains the same basic thought as "firstfruits of those who are asleep," namely the union which exists between Christ and believers in the experience of resurrection. At the same time it expresses more definitely than I Corinthians 15:20-23 the uniqueness and preeminence, the headship, of Christ in this solidaric relationship. Taken together, these two passages teach that "the firstfruits of those who are asleep," "the firstborn from the dead," "the beginning," "the one who is first," and "the head" all describe the *second Adam as resurrected.*

I Corinthians 15:12-19

A careful reading of I Corinthians 15 will reveal that the whole argument rests almost entirely on the firstfruits "thesis" of verse 20.[25] This can be seen in part in verses 12-19. Here Paul has not yet come to the ringing affirmation of Christ's resurrection made in verse 20 "But now . . ." (νυνὶ δέ). Accordingly, he reasons hypothetically. On the one hand,

opened up the way. With him the great Resurrection became reality. And very similar is the meaning of Firstborn from the dead: he ushers in the world of the resurrection" (Ridderbos, *Paul*, p. 56). Cf. p. 538; *Kolossenzen*, p. 143.
21. Cf. Käsemann, "Taufliturgie," p. 42; Bornkamm, "Häresie," p. 139.
22. Cf. Michaelis, *TDNT*, 6:882.
23. So Ridderbos, *Paul*, pp. 376-387.
24. Ridderbos himself stresses this (*Paul*, pp. 386f.).
25. Cf. Herman, *Kyrios und Pneuma*, p. 62: "The entire chapter speaks of Christ's resurrection and its connection with the resurrection of Christians."

he argues from the resurrection of Christ to the resurrection of believers: if Christ has been raised, then the proclamation of general resurrection cannot be called into question (v. 12). Similarly, to deny Christ's resurrection, in effect denies the resurrection of believers. Such a denial, if true, means that Paul's preaching is empty (v. 14) and the faith of his hearers empty and futile (vv. 14, 17). It means that believers are still in their sins (v. 17), that those who are dead have perished (v. 18) and that those who are living are objects for special pity (v. 19). On the other hand, he can reverse the line of argument by reasoning directly from a denial of the resurrection of believers to a denial of the resurrection of Christ (vv. 13, 15, 16).

Two factors stand out rather clearly in this argumentation: (1) Throughout the governing presupposition is the unity of the resurrection of Christ and the resurrection of believers. The one cannot be had without the other; indeed the one is given with the other. Consequently, belief in the one necessarily implies belief in the other.[26] Without this underlying notion of unity the apostle's statements are so much empty rhetoric. (2) Paul reasons in either direction, from (the denial of) the resurrection of believers to (the denial of) the resurrection of Christ, as well as the reverse. This shows just how firm and close in his mind is the bond between the two resurrections; he views them not so much as separate occurrences as two episodes of the same event.

II Corinthians 4:14

In the context (vv. 7ff.) Paul spells out the suffering involved in his gospel ministry. This brings him in verse 14 to a confession of the faith (cf. v. 13) which sustains him in these trials, a confession which runs in part: "The one who raised the Lord Jesus will also raise us with Jesus." In this declaration both the unity of the two resurrections and the temporal distinction between them stand out clearly. Admittedly the notion of future resurrection "with Jesus" ($\sigma\grave{\upsilon}\nu$ ᾽Ιη-σοῦ), taken by itself, is difficult, but intelligible if taken with the idea of Christ as the "firstfruits." At any rate, there are no grounds for qualifying the concept of future resurrection,

---

26. Cf. R. Koch, "L'aspect eschatologique de l'Esprit du Seigneur d'après saint Paul," *Studiorum Paulinorum congressus internationalis Catholicus—1961*, Analecta Biblica, 17 (Rome: Pontifical Biblical Institute, 1963), 1:134; cf. p. 140.

either in the direction of some conception of contemporaneity (a notion excluded by the future tense), or by toning down the force of the σύν so that the thought becomes "resurrection in communion with Jesus" or "as a benefit of this communion" or even "resurrection in order to be with Jesus."[27] The thought of this verse—or at least a thought similar to it—is probably also present in I Thessalonians 4:14.

THE RESURRECTION OF CHRIST AND THE PAST RESURRECTION OF THE BELIEVER

The verses considered so far stress the organic connection between the resurrection of Jesus and the future, bodily resurrection of believers. To conclude, however, that the soteric significance of the latter lies only in this tie grasps only half the picture and so misses the whole. We must now take into account those places where Paul says that the believer has *already* been raised with Christ. This thought is expressed most pointedly in Ephesians 2:5f.; Colossians 2:12f.; 3:1; Romans 6:3ff. and Galatians 2:19f.

Ephesians 2:5, 6

The single problem to be faced now in this and related passages concerns the temporal reference of the verb "to raise with" (συνεγείρω) and other closely associated verbs in the aorist tense. Specifically, do they refer solely to what took place in the historical experience of Christ or do they apply as well to what has happened in the actual life experience of the individual believer? Note that this question does not posit a disjunction. For, in view of the significance of Christ's resurrection as the "firstfruits," a reflection on solidarity with him in his emergence from the tomb can hardly be eliminated from these expressions.[28] The issue then is whether something more is in view. Is Paul referring as well to a specific occurrence in the actual experience of the believer?

27. An overview of various renderings is provided by H. Windisch, *Der zweite Korintherbrief*, MeyerK, 6, 9th ed. (Göttingen: Vandenhoeck & Ruprecht, 1924), pp. 149f.

28. On this point Rudolf Schnackenburg, who finds here a reference to what takes place in baptism, overstates: "Thereby all attempts at explanation fall away which want to shift the statements of Eph. 2:5f. back into the historical place of the great Christ-event" (*Das Heilsgeschehen bei der Taufe nach dem Apostel Paulus*, Münchner Theologische Studien, I. historische Abteilung, 1. Band (Munich: Karl Zink, 1950), p. 70).

Within Reformed exegesis, opinion is divided along geographical lines, so far as representative figures are concerned. The Dutch exegetes emphasize the presence of the redemptive-historical aspect to the exclusion of individual, experiential considerations. Ridderbos, for instance, comments on verses 4-6: "From the final words it appears unmistakably that Paul again thinks christologically and redemptive-historically and not in terms of anthropology and the *ordo salutis.*"[29] On the other hand, British-American interpretation, while recognizing an allusion to solidarity with Christ in his historical work, maintains that Paul's distinguishing interest here is the transformation of the individual.[30]

While the language employed surely reflects Paul's redemptive-historical outlook in these verses, the conclusion that he is describing what has taken place for believers existentially is difficult to avoid. The enlivening and resurrection spoken of refer directly to the death mentioned in verse 5a. Clearly this "being dead" is not solidaric involvement with Christ in his death, for it is "being dead in transgressions." In view is the actual, existential deadness of Paul and his readers. The verses immediately preceding confirm this point. Verse 5a together with verse 4 resumes the thought begun in verse 1 which was temporally interrupted. Verses 2 and 3 are a parenthetical insertion, expanding on the transgressions and sins mentioned in verse 1 and so upon the transgressions in verse 5. Specifically, they provide an extended description of the former moral depravity and guilt of Paul and his readers.[31] Among other things, they "walked" or conducted themselves according to the standards of this evil (cf. Gal. 1:4) age, according to the spirit of disobedience (v. 2); they "walked" in the lusts of the flesh, by doing the desires of the flesh (v. 3). Such language requires that the

---

29. *Paul*, p. 211; cf. J. A. C. Van Leeuwen, *Paulus' Zendbrieven aan Efeze, Colosse, Filemon, en Thessalonika*, KNT, 10 (Amsterdam: Van Bottenburg, 1926), p. 53; Grosheide, *Efeziers*, p. 39.
30. So Simpson, *Ephesians*, pp. 51f.; W. Hendriksen, *New Testament Commentary. Exposition of Ephesians* (Grand Rapids: Baker, 1967), pp. 116-118; C. Hodge, *A Commentary on the Epistle to the Ephesians* (New York: Robert Carter, 1856), pp. 112-116; J. Eadie, *A Commentary on the Greek Text of the Epistle of Paul to the Ephesians*, 3rd ed. (Edinburgh: T. & T. Clark, 1883), p. 142.
31. Note the shift in subject from verse 2 to verse 3, as well as the parallel shift in verses 1 and 5a. This is an indication of the paradigmatic nature of the discussion: all believers are in view.

deadness mentioned in verse 5 not only involves 'but refers primarily to individual moral depravity. Consequently, the enlivening and resurrection (vv. 5f.), which took place *when*[32] they were dead as just defined, at least includes the initial experience of transformation and ethical renewal.[33]

Further, in verse 10, the enlivening and resurrection with Christ mentioned in verses 5f. are described as being "created in Christ Jesus" (cf. II Cor. 5:17). The express purpose of this new creation in Christ is "good works, which God prepared beforehand that we should walk in them." "Walking" here is a key word, specifying the integrating theme in this section (vv. 1-10). Having begun with a reference to a "walk" in trespasses and sins, Paul ends by mentioning its counterpart, a "walk" in good works. Accordingly, the decisive pivot of this experiential reversal, effecting this about-face in "walk," is being raised with Christ.

Conclusion. In verse 6, resurrection with Christ refers to the transition in the actual life history of the individual Christian from being by nature an object of wrath (v. 3) to becoming a recipient of God's mercy and love (v. 4). While the apostle's perspectives are certainly *heilshistorisch,* his primary interest is decidedly *heilsordelijk.*[34]

Colossians 2:12, 13; 3:1

Colossians 2:12, 13 is written from a redemptive-historical, christological outlook. Nevertheless, as in Ephesians 2:5, 6 the aspect of individual, existential appropriation is also present. Two considerations make this clear.

(1) There are several parallels between these verses and Ephesians 2:5f., which are particular instances of the broad, genetic connection between the two letters.[35] Specifically, Colossians 2:12, 13f. is the only other place where Paul both

32. The participle ὄντας has a temporal or circumstantial force.
33. In view of these considerations it is difficult to understand Van Leeuwen's insistence (*Zendbrieven*, p. 53) that Paul does not take up the matter of individual renovation until verse 13.
34. J. Murray's comment bearing on these verses is well worth noting here: "Furthermore, it is too apparent to need demonstration that the historic events of Calvary and the resurrection from Joseph's tomb do not register the changes which are continuously being wrought when the people of God are translated from the power of darkness into Christ's kingdom of life, liberty, and peace" ("Definitive Sanctification," p. 17).
35. This connection enjoys virtually universal recognition (although it is frequently coupled with a denial of the Pauline authorship of Ephesians); cf. Ridderbos, *Kolossenzen*, pp. 112f.; Hendricksen, *Ephesians*, pp. 5-32.

uses συνζωοποιέω and combines it with συνεγείρω. Also, the qualification of the object of the main verb in verse 13 (συν-εζωοποίησεν), "you when you were dead in your trans-gressions," is almost identical with the language in Ephesians 2:1 and 5.[36] Hence, the thought is also the same: being raised with Christ and being made alive with him[37] refer to deadness defined in terms which include moral depravity, and so describe at least some facet of the believer's initial saving experience.

2) The prepositional phrase "through faith" (διὰ τῆς πίστεως) (v. 12) is clearly an adverbial qualification of the verb συνηγέρθητε. Believers have been raised with Christ through faith. Paul is not saying here what he might have said, that resurrection with Christ took place in the garden of Joseph and this fact is subsequently registered by faith. Rather he relates faith to the *experience* of being raised with Christ in a pointedly *instrumental* fashion.

The only other occurrence of συνεγείρω is in Colossians 3:1, where it has the same force as the identical form (συνηγέρθητε) in 2:12. In the immediate context Paul makes being raised with Christ the realized condition and so the basis for the exhortation given in general terms in the apodosis of verse 1 and in verse 2, and developed in more specific fashion through to 4:6. In other words, having been raised with Christ, together with its concomitants (cf. esp. v. 3; 2:20), are the grounds for a lengthy paraenetic discourse. Accordingly, the protasis in verse 1 can hardly refer only to solidarity with Christ at the time of his resurrection. In that case, there would be either an inexplicable gap in his argu-ment or a flat contradiction with his ethical teaching else-where.[38] Apparently in this instance as well resurrection with Christ is primarily the initial soteric experience of the individual, including moral renovation.

Romans 6:3ff.

Our primary interest in this much-discussed passage is to

---

36. "and the uncircumcision of your flesh," which immediately follows, is a divergence from the language of Ephesians 2. However, it confirms rather forcefully that Paul has in mind the aspect of moral impotence and pollution; cf. Ridderbos, *Kolossenzen*, pp. 182f. The use of the possessive pronoun strengthens this point.

37. Note that the sequence of the two verbs is the reverse of Ephesians 2:5f., an indication that here, as there, they are used synonymously; cf. Rom. 8:11; I Cor. 15:22; Rom. 4:17.

38. See Murray's statement quoted above, note 34.

trace its development of the notion of resurrection with Christ as an historical, yet experiential reality. While this idea is not stated quite so explicitly here, it can be seen rather easily against the background of the passages just discussed, particularly Colossians 2:11-13 with its common appeal to the significance of baptism.

To the objection, raised in an interrogatory fashion in 6:1,[39] that the doctrines of grace the apostle has just been developing (cf. esp. 5:12-21) encourage a life of sin, Paul counters, likewise in the form of a question, with the thesis that believers "have died to sin" (v. 2). This thesis supplies the premise fundamental to the rest of the lengthy section (6:1—7:6).[40] Paul's primary concern in this passage, then, is *heilsordelijk*, with the matters of existential sinning, a sinful way of life,[41] and the believer's death to the sin in view. The death to sin spoken of here has taken place in the life history of the individual believer.[42] At the same time, however, redemptive-historical considerations are also present and play an important role in the argument. This passage, as in the passages already examined, cannot be considered either/ or.

Beginning with verse 3 Paul proceeds to expand and validate his thesis that the believer has died to sin by appealing to the significance of baptism (only the basic elements of this appeal need concern us here). Baptism is "into Christ" (cf. Gal. 3:27); that is, baptism signifies union with Christ.[43] This union is understood in a quite concrete manner. It is union with Christ in all phases of his messianic work and all that he is by virtue of this work. Hence baptism into Christ means union with him in his death (vv. 3, 4a, 5a; cf. "We died with Christ," v. 8; II Tim. 2:11; "Our old man was crucified with him," v. 6; Gal. 2:19) and burial ("We were buried with him," v. 4; cf. Col. 2:12). Thus Paul's central thesis is established: Believers are united with Christ in his death; his death was specifically a death to sin (cf. v. 10); therefore believers here died to sin.

---

39. Whether this question takes up an actual objection or is rhetorical is a point which need not concern us here.
40. Cf. Murray, *Romans*, 1:213; "Definitive Sanctification," pp. 6f.
41. The verbs "are we to continue" (v. 1) and "shall we live" (v. 2) serve to accent this.
42. Cf. Murray, "Definitive Sanctification," p. 17.
43. Cf. Gal. 3:26-28; I Cor. 12:13 with v. 27; Rom. 12:4f.

The latter part of verse 4 expresses for the first time the important positive implication of Paul's fundamental premise and so brings into view that feature of the passage most germane to our discussion. Strictly speaking, death to sin is not an adequate description of the believer's existence, because it has only negative force. The believer is one united with Christ in his death and burial "in order that as Christ was raised from the dead through the glory of the Father, so we too might walk in newness of life."

The theme of resurrection with Christ is plain in this clause, especially as one grasps the underlying pattern of thought. Really more basic than the thesis that the believer has died to sin is the notion of union with Christ in the various phases of his messianic experience. Hence Paul's line of reasoning is as follows: On the one hand, as Christ died (to sin), so believers by virtue of union with him in his death have died (to sin); on the other hand, as Christ was raised from the dead, so believers by virtue of union with him in his resurrection have been raised from the dead. Because of the solidarity between Christ and believers, the inseparability of resurrection from death in the case of the former means their inseparability in the experience of the latter.

That verse 4c does not utilize specifically the vocabulary of resurrection is explained by the controlling question posed in verse 1. "Walking in newness of life" is a more appropriate and much more pointed contrast to "remaining in sin" than "having been raised with Christ." Nevertheless, as just indicated, resurrection with Christ is the underlying, structural consideration.[44]

Verse 4c, then, shows rather graphically that Paul views resurrection with Christ not only in terms of solidarity with him at the time-point of his resurrection but also as part of a decisive transition in the lifetime of the individual believer. If only the former were the case, Paul would be arguing directly from the once-for-all event of Christ's resurrection to the believer's new walk, and this would involve an hiatus completely foreign to the controlling interest and structure of thought in the immediate and broader context (6:1—7:6). Paul's primary and repeated stress is that death with Christ

---

44. This correlation between the believer's new "walk" and his co-resurrection is another indication of affinity with Ephesians 2:1-10; cf. above, p. 43.

(to sin and to the law) includes an experiential aspect which excludes the possibility of continuing in the bondage and practice of sin. Accordingly, resurrection with Christ likewise involves an existential component. The believer's continuing walk in newness of life is based upon resurrection with Christ as that has taken place in his actual life history.

A further consideration here is that for Paul "life" in the soteriological sense[45] does not have an indefinite basis and character. Rather it is grounded specifically in the resurrection of Jesus and its manifestation is always an expression of that resurrection. Life for Paul is pointedly resurrection-life. This is plain in the present context. That life which Christ now lives "to God" (v. 10), he lives as "raised from the dead" (v. 9). Accordingly, by virtue of union with him, as believers reckon themselves dead to sin and alive "to God" (v. 11), they are to present themselves "to God as alive from the dead" (v. 13). The thought of co-resurrection, then, cannot be excluded from verse 4c.

Verse 5 explains the bond established in verse 4 between Christ's resurrection and the believers' walk in newness of life.[46] "For if we have been united with him in the likeness of his death, we will certainly also be united with him (in the likeness) of his resurrection." The syntactical difficulties of this statement need not detain us here. The consensus of Protestant interpretation is that: (1) "united with" (σύμφυτοι) is to be joined directly with "the likeness" (τῷ ὁμοιώματι)[47] and (2) the latter is to be read in verse 5b where ellipsis has occurred.[48] The substructure of this one-sentence argument is not difficult to detect. "The underlying thought is again the inseparable conjunction of Christ's death and resurrection, and the inference drawn from this conjunction is that if we are united with Christ in his death we must be also in his resurrection. Disjunction in our case is as impossible as disjunction in his."[49] While the language here may be different

---

45. A nonsoteric usage also occurs; e.g., I Cor. 15:19, 45a.

46. Cf. Ridderbos, *Romeinen*, p. 127; note the conjunction "for" (γάρ).

47. Roman Catholic interpreters usually read an αὐτῷ from verse 4a with σύμφυτοι and take τῷ ὁμοιώματι as an instrumental dative referring to baptism; cf. Schnackenburg, *Heilsgeschehen*, p. 41 and the literature cited there (n. 131).

48. So, e.g., Murray, *Romans*, 1:218f.; Ridderbos, *Romeinen*, pp. 127f.; P. Althaus, *Der Brief an die Römer*, NTD, 6 (Göttingen: Vandenhoeck & Ruprecht, 1966), p. 62.

49. Murray, *Romans*, 1:218. The word used to express union with Christ, the *hapax legomenon* σύμφυτοι, derives from a root (συμφύομαι) meaning to "grow together" (cf. W. Grundmann, *TDNT*, 7:786), and so expresses rather pointedly the notion of solidarity. It would be wrong to read the idea of growth or process into the verse on

than in Ephesians 2:6 and Colossians 2:12 the basic thought is the same: believers have been raised with Christ.[50]

One feature in this verse requires further attention. Believers are joined to the *likeness* of Christ's death and resurrection. This is an indication that Paul has something more or something other in view than union with Christ at the time-points of his death, burial, and resurrection. Without compromising the strongly-expressed notion of solidarity, "likeness" introduces an element of distinction (cf. Rom. 8:3; Phil. 2:7).[51] What this additional or discriminating element is emerges in the light of the main emphasis of the context. Believers have died to sin, and this death is an actual experience of believers (v. 2). Accordingly, their resurrection invariably conjoined with this death is likewise understood in an existential fashion (v. 4). Now since *this* death and resurrection is in view, that is, death and resurrection which has taken place in the life history of the believer, the struc-

the basis of this form, as if death with Christ to sin were progressivley realized. The pivotal and sustained emphasis in the context on the definitiveness of the breach with sin excludes any such notion. The sole point is "the intimacy of the union involved" (Murray, p. 218). Ridderbos (p. 127) translates with "incorporated"; Grundmann with "belonging together," "united with."

50. The future tense in verse 5b has logical force and expresses certainty (cf. Murray, *Romans*, 1:219; Ridderbos, *Romeinen*, p. 129; cf. also ζήσομεν as the preferred reading in v. 2). W. Thüsing (*Per Christum in Deum. Studien zum Verhältnis von Christozentrik und Theozentrik in den paulinischen Hauptbriefen*, NA, Nene Folge, 1 [Münster: Aschendorff, 1965], pp. 139-144) argues at length for a temporal force. In my opinion, however, he does not succeed finally in overcoming what he himself recognizes (p. 141) to be the basic difficulty with this position: how a future indicative (v. 5b) can be made the basis for a present imperative (v. 4c). He appeals to the broader structure of Paul's theology, principally the bond between (present) righteousness and (future) glory. But in so doing he overlooks one of the more important structural characteristics of the immediate context: life (wherever it be found) is always exponential of the experience of resurrection (cf. esp. v. 13).

51. ". . . distance along with all similarity . . ." (Ridderbos, *Romeinen*, p. 129). Ridderbos also suggests that this force of ὁμοίωμα is anticipated by ὥσπερ in v. 4 (p. 127). R. C. Tannehill (*Dying and Rising with Christ. A Study in Pauline Theology*, Beiheft zur Zeitschrift für die neutestamentliche Wissenschaft und die Kunde der alteren Kirche, 32, ed. W. Eltester [Berlin: Töpelmann, 1967], pp. 7-43) argues (pp. 35-39), primarily on the basis of Phil. 2:7, that for Paul ὁμοίωμα is synonymous with μορφή and that hence the former expresses identity ("the form of the reality itself in its outward appearance," p. 35) rather than likeness. Entirely apart from his treatment of the usage in Phil. 2:7 and Rom. 8:3, which, in my opinion, is at least open to question, it is difficult to see how this force fits in Romans 6:5. His conclusion that ὁμοίωμα is part of the vocabulary of a "theology of metamorphosis" (p. 37) found in Rom. 8:29; II Cor. 3:18; Phil. 3:21 encounters insurmountable problems in this context. In Romans 6:1ff. "dying and rising with Christ" is not a motif expressing the *process* of transformation or gradual conformity to Christ; rather the sustained emphasis is on the definitive breach with sin which lies in the believer's past.

ture of this experience cannot be identical with Christ's. To cite just one difference, the former lacks the somatic aspect which is an essential characteristic of the latter.[52] Apparently, then, Paul is reflecting on these differences in verse 5. And his use of "likeness" confirms rather pointedly that the solidarity with Christ in his resurrection described here is an experience in the life of the individual believer.

In verse 6 the co-resurrection of the new man (cf. Col. 3:9f. with 3:1; Eph. 4:22-24) is the implied contrast to the crucifixion of the old man with Christ. Since this notion of co-crucifixion is clearly correlate with the primary emphasis in the context on the believer's death with Christ to sin,[53] it too has an existential reference. Verse 6 confirms this by anticipating the destruction of "the body of sin"[54] and cessation of bondage to sin as direct results of co-crucifixion. It follows, then, that the bondage to righteousness implied in the latter part of the verse (cf. vv. 16, 18, 19, 22) presupposes co-resurrection as an experiential reality. Also, in the parallelism of verse 13, for believers to present their members as instruments of righteousness is for them to present themselves as "alive from the dead." The thought here, close to that of Colossians 3:1, is fairly paraphrased: present yourselves to God as those who have been raised (existentially) (with Christ; cf. vv. 10f.) from the dead.[55]

Similarly in verse 8 living with Christ [56] is difficult to understand other than in an existential sense. The close parallel with verse 5 in structure as well as in thought is apparent, so

---

52. Cf. Murray, *Romans*, 1:218. Verse 12 makes this point clear. There Paul says, in effect, to his readers: "the resurrection you have experienced has taken place 'in your mortal body.'"
53. "Knowing this" indicates that verse 6 is a further development of what precedes, particularly the protasis in verse 5.
54. The thought is the destruction of the body "as conditioned and controlled by sin" (Murray, *Romans*, 1:220).
55. Ridderbos maintains that the contrast between the old and new man is to be understood, "not in the first place in the sense of the *ordo salutis*, but in that of the history of redemption; . . . not first of all in a personal and ethical sense, but in a redemptive-historical, eschatological sense" (*Paul*, p. 63; cf. *Romeinen*, p. 129). To be sure, the language employed by Paul reflects his redemptive-historical perspective, and Ridderbos apparently does not consider the interests he contrasts mutually exclusive (cf., however, *Paul*, p. 208). Still, as I have tried to show above, in verse 6, this context as a whole, and others, Paul's primary emphasis is on the *ordo salutis*, on the radical transition effected in the life history of the individual believer.
56. The verb "we will live" (συζήσομεν) is a logical future expressing certainty, although a temporal force is naturally also present (so Murray, *Romans*, 1:203; Ridderbos, *Romeinen*, p. 131).

that in view of the invariable connection between resurrection and life (cf. esp. vv. 9f.), living with Christ as an individual, experiential reality presupposes an inception of that state, a co-resurrection, of the same order.

Before leaving this passage, one point already noted along with several of its implications needs to be stressed. In establishing his central thesis that believers have died to sin, Paul does not argue directly from their involvement in Christ's death. Rather his death is their death because they are united to *him*. Baptism is into his death because baptism is "into Christ Jesus" (v. 3). In other words, union with Christ is the basic conception; only because believers are joined to him as he is by virtue of his death (crucifixion, burial, and resurrection) can they be said to participate in these events, to have died with him, and so forth.

Two further sets of observations amplify this point:

(1) The union, the being joined to Christ in view here is primarily *experiential* (*heilsordelijk*) in nature. It is a union which is constitutive as well as descriptive of the actual existence of the individual believer. To be sure, the range of the Pauline "in Christ" is much broader than the actual life histories of individual believers. It is eternal in scope. Believers have been chosen "in him before the foundation of the world" (Eph. 1:4; cf. Rom. 8:29). And almost every one of the passages already examined indicate in some way the solidarity of believers with Christ in the past, definitive, historical experiences of the latter. But neither the predestinarian "in Christ" nor the redemptive-historical "in Christ" eclipse the distinctiveness of the existential "in Christ."

This experiential aspect is present in Romans 6:3ff. wherever crucifixion, death, burial, resurrection, or life with Christ are mentioned. As we have tried to show, these references describe the actual life experience of the individual believer. Therefore the union basic to this experience, of which this experience is an expression, is likewise experiential. The distinctness of this conception of experiential union is clearly expressed in Paul's description of baptism as baptism *into* Christ (v. 3). Baptism signifies and seals a *transition* in the experience of the recipient, a transition from being (existentially) apart from Christ to being (existentially) joined to him. Galatians 3:27 is even more graphic: "Those who have been baptized into Christ have put on Christ" (cf. I Cor. 12:13).[57]

Union with Christ as an experiential reality is also distinguished rather clearly in Ephesians 2:12 where Paul says that the Ephesian Christians, chosen in Christ before the foundation of the world (1:4), were "at that time separated (χωρίς) from Christ." "Formerly" (vv. 11, 13) and "at that time" (v. 12) hardly have a different reference than "formerly" in verses 2 and 3. The Christless, alien state described in the immediate context of verse 12 coincides with the "walk" in trespasses and sins mentioned in verses 1ff. Consequently, the transition described in verses 5f. as being made alive with Christ, etc. pivots on being joined to Christ in an existential sense. The variations of the "in Christ" formula used repeatedly to describe the state resultant upon this transition confirm this experiential sense (vv. 6, 7, 10, 13, 15, 22). The transition from being an object of God's wrath (v. 3) to experiencing his love (v. 4) takes place at the point of being joined (existentially) to Christ.

Similarly, the effectual call of the gospel is a call *into* personal communion (εἰς κοινωνίαν) with Christ (I Cor. 1:9).[58] And the immediate end of having died to the law through the body of Christ for the purpose of bearing fruit to God is being joined (εἰς τὸ γενέσθαι) to the resurrected Christ (Rom. 7:4).

There is no element in the whole of Paul's soteriology more basic than this existential union with Christ. To treat it in abstraction from or to the exclusion of the ideas that believers have been chosen eternally in Christ and were contemplated as one with Christ at the time of his sufferings, death and resurrection would of course radically distort Paul's perspective. The predestinarian, the past historical and the existential "in Christ" are indissolubly connected. The former two, each in its own way, are the basis for and give rise to the latter. But precisely this organic bond, this inseparability, makes equivocation in dealing with Paul's teaching on union with Christ a subtle danger to which the interpretation of Paul is constantly exposed. Falling upon the

---

57. ". . . the phrase describes the manner of entering upon the state of being-in-Christ. Those who are baptized *into* Christ are those who afterwards are *in* Christ" (E. Best, *One Body in Christ* [London: S. P. C. K., 1955], p. 73).
58. "Although they had been chosen in Christ before times eternal, yet they were Christless until they were called effectually into the fellowship of God's Son (I Cor. 1:9)" (Murray, *Redemption: Accomplished and Applied*, p. 205).

Scylla of equivocation may not be so serious an error as ship-wreck on the Charybdis of isolation or exclusion; however, the former can hardly fail to produce a confused understanding of Paul. For, as we have seen and will continue to see, in Paul's soteriology the realization of redemption in the experience of the individual, both in its inception and in its continuation, is based on the *experience* of being joined to Christ.

(2) Reflection on the fundamental role of union with Christ in Romans 6:3ff. not only discloses its primarily experiential force there, but also that the (existential) crucifixion, death, burial and resurrection mentioned are not distinct or separate occurrences in the experience of the individual believer. Each is not a separate stage in an *ordo salutis* but an aspect of the single, indivisible event of being joined to Christ experientially. This needs to be kept in view continuously in discussing the idea of being raised with Christ. The latter is always exponential of the experience of incorporation. Romans 7:4 makes this clear. The positive end interposed between having died to the law (as the instrument of sin, v. 13) through the body of Christ and bearing fruit to God (cf. v. 6 with 6:4c) is not being raised with Christ but being joined to him as the one who has been raised.

Galatians 2:19, 20

The notion of resurrection with Christ is not difficult to see in these verses. Their affinity especially with the passage in Romans 6:3ff. appears at several points. Verse 20 contains the only other reference in Paul to crucifixion with Christ (cf. Rom. 6:6). Having died "that I might live to God" (v. 19b) is reminiscent of Romans 6:10f. The death to the law spoken of (v. 19a) is correlative with death to sin (cf. Rom. 7:4, 6 with 6:6, 18, 22). Therefore, since this death is described in terms of solidarity with Christ in his crucifixion, the life which forms its pointed contrast (v. 20) should be understood in terms of solidarity in his resurrection. Moreover, since this life is obviously life in individual, existential union with Christ ("Christ in me"), the co-crucifixion and the co-resurrection in view are likewise primarily experiential in nature.

In these verses Paul writes in the singular,[59] using himself

---

59. "The only place where Paul personally designates himself the object of Christ's love and devotion!" (Schnackenburg, *Heilsgeschehen*, p. 60, n. 201).

and his experience as illustrative of all believers.[60] This justifies understanding the "we" statements in the other passages examined distributively and as applying individually to every believer.

The Union Involved

In this section our concern has been with Paul's teaching that believers have been raised with Christ, particularly with the question *when* this resurrection took place. This may appear to be an unnecessary question: if believers were raised with Christ, the time can only be when he himself was raised. However, such reasoning grasps only half the matter. For in speaking of the believer's past resurrection with Christ, Paul has in view as well an experience in the actual life history of the believer. In fact, in passages such as Ephesians 2:5f. and Romans 6:3ff. this experiential aspect is his primary interest; in the latter, his sustained, developed interest. Specifically, being raised with Christ is an aspect of being joined to him existentially, so that what holds true for resurrection simply reflects the broader, more basic notion of union. Here again a warning against the opposite dangers of equivocation and abstract separation is in order. "It is necessary to stress both aspects, the past historical and the experiential in their distinctness, on the one hand, and in their inter-dependence, on the other."[61]

Much of recent Pauline interpretation has failed to maintain this required balance. For the most part, imbalance has tended toward blurring the distinctness and definitiveness of the past historical character of Christ's (death and) resurrection.[62] Primarily on the basis of an appeal to Romans 6:1-11, this tendency has taken form either in the notion that in baptism the death of Christ *as an event* is made present in the experience of the recipient,[63] or in the idea that in the sacra-

60. Note in the unit of material (vv. 15-21) the shift in subject from plural to singular without any break in the argument.
61. Murray, "Definitive Sanctification," p. 19.
62. For a summary of this trend cf. esp. Ridderbos, *Paul*, pp. 406-410.
63. This view is characteristic of the so-called mystery-theology found primarily in Roman Catholic circles; so, e.g., O. Kuss, who defends as Pauline "the thesis of a sacramental 'actualization,' 'representation' of the salvation-event in baptism" (*Der Römerbrief* [Regensburg: Friedrich Pustet, 1959], p. 311); cf. the literature cited on pp. 318f. This interpretation draws heavily on the conclusion of the older "history-of-religions" school that in his teaching on the sacraments Paul has been strongly influenced by the ritual practices of contemporary mystery cults. For a thorough investigation and rejection of the thesis of a positive connection between Paul and

ment all temporal and spatial distinctions are eliminated so
that the believer becomes contemporaneous with Christ's
death and resurrection.[64] The former conception, so far as it
seeks support in Romans 6:3ff., runs counter to Paul's
repeated references to Christ's death in the aorist tense; it
also fails to make the distinction required by the word
"likeness" (v. 5).[65] The idea of contemporaneity basic to the
latter rests, in turn, upon presuppositions concerning the
nature of history derived from post-Kantian thinking not only
foreign but inimical to Paul.[66]

However, assuming that Paul does not compromise the
definitiveness of Christ's past historical work, what is the
relationship between the respective experience of Christ and
the believer? How are we to understand the interdependence of experience which is temporally distinct yet
described in terms of co-resurrection? John Murray for-
mulated the problem with characteristic sharpness:

> Admittedly it is difficult to define the precise relations of the past
> historical to the continuously operative. . . . To put it more ac-
> curately, it is difficult to determine how the finished action of
> Christ in the past relates itself to those who are contemplated in
> that action prior to the time when that past action takes effect in
> their life history.[67]

the hellenistic mystery religions on this and related points, cf. G. Wagner, *Pauline
Baptism and the Pagan Mysteries*, trans. J. P. Smith (Edinburgh: Oliver & Boyd,
1967); cf. also J. Gresham Machen, *The Origin of Paul's Religion* (New York: Mac-
millan, 1928), pp. 280-290.
64. This view in one form or another characterizes most Protestant interpretation.
Its fullest statement has been given by W. T. Hahn, *Das Mitsterben und Mitaufserste-
ben mit Christus bei Paulus* (Gütersloh: C. Bertelsmann, 1937). With a conscious
appeal to the thought of Kierkegaard, Hahn seeks to show that Paul teaches an "incorporation into and contemporization [Vergleichzeitigung] with the Christ-event"
(p. 114); cf. p. 175: "In the Christ-event the category of time is suspended [aufge-
hoben]." Cf. the similar conclusion reached by F. Neugebauer, "Das Paulinische 'In
Christo.'" *New Testament Studies*, 4 (1957-58): 138 and *In Christus. Eine Untersuchung
zum Paulinischen Glaubenverständnis* (Göttingen: Vandenhoeck & Ruprecht, 1961), p.
148.
65. Cf. Ridderbos, *Paul*, p. 408, n. 45.
66. This interpretation is controlled rather thoroughly by the idea of *Geschichte* cur-
rent in much contemporary theology; cf. esp. Barth's insistence upon recognition of
"the simultaneity of the one act of salvation" (*Church Dogmatics*, trans. G. W.
Bromiley (Edinburgh, T. & T. Clark, 1958), IV, 2:503. Cf. also Neugebauer's
appeal to Heidegger (*New Testament Studies*, 4:138, n. 1).
67. "Definitive Sanctification," p. 20.

And Herman Ridderbos writes:

> . . . in the epistles of Paul that have come down to us this relation-
> ship of having been included in Christ in the redemptive-
> historical and predestinarian sense and sacramental incorporation
> into (the body of) Christ and thus into his death and resurrection,
> is not expressly treated or explained. We are left to conclusions,
> therefore, which we must draw ourselves, with all the difficulties
> and dangers of such a procedure.[68]

Despite the difficulties involved here, interpretation is
faced with the task of articulating this interrelatedness as
precisely as Paul's statements permit. Writing on Romans
6:1-11, Murray provides this formally precise statement:

> This sustained introduction of the once-for-all past historical in a
> context that clearly deals with what occurs actually and prac-
> tically in the life history of individuals makes inevitable the inter-
> pretation that the past historical conditions the continuously
> existential, not simply as laying the basis for it and as providing
> the analogy in the realm of the past historical for what continues
> to occur in the realm of our experience, but conditions the latter
> for the reason that something occurred in the past historical
> which makes necessary what is realized and exemplified in the
> actual life history of these same persons.[69]

It would be difficult to find a better summary of our
findings in this section or a more discriminating expression of
the balance of continuities and discontinuities indicated by
the "likeness" of Romans 6:5: "Something occurred in the
past historical which makes necessary what is realized and
exemplified in the actual life history." This captures Paul's
conception which relates Christ's past to the believer's
present without compromising the definitiveness of the
former or reducing it to a bare analogy or necessary but ext-
rinsic basis of the latter. What further can be said about
Paul's understanding of this structural bond, this organic unity, particularly as it involves the experience of resurrection?

In recent decades the idea of corporate personality has
been widely used to explain Paul's understanding of the

---

68. *Paul*, p. 406.
69. "Definitive Sanctification," p. 19. Cf. Ridderbos, *When The Time Had Fully
Come*, p. 58: "Whatever happened to Christ, happened to the Church, not only
analogously or metaphorically, but in the historical sense of the word."

solidaric relationship between Christ and believers.[70] Frequently, however, it obscures rather than clarifies problems.[71] This appears to be the case, for instance, with Ridderbos, when he explains the interdependence of the history of redemption and the experience of the believer in terms of the notion of corporate personality:

> The corporate idea of the all-in-One derived from the significance of Adam—thus we may conclude—works itself out in all sorts of ways in the Pauline explication of the redemptive event that made its appearance in Christ. It teaches us to understand the redemptive-historical character not only of that which has once occurred in Christ, but also of the way in which those who belong to Christ participate once and continuously in the salvation wrought in Christ.[72]

The problem is not with these statements but with the use of the idea of corporate personality in the immediate context to brush aside in one sentence the problematics of the "realistic-federal" debate which has structured to such a great extent traditional Reformed interpretation of Paul's conceptions of solidarity.[73] The result is a certain vagueness in Ridderbos's own usage. Perhaps the traditional problematics can be transcended or otherwise improved upon or perhaps even shown to be false, but to explain how the notion of corporate personality does this would require more careful demonstration than Ridderbos has provided.

So far as our discussion here is concerned, we confine ourselves to observing that the term "corporate personality" may be used to describe Paul's understanding of Christ in his solidarity with believers on the following stipulations:

(1) Recognition must be given to *all* the aspects of this

---

70. The term "corporate personality" is apparently used for the first time by H. Wheeler Robinson in a 1936 essay, "The Hebrew Conception of Corporate Personality" (reprinted in H. W. Robinson, *Corporate Personality in Ancient Israel*, Facet Books, Biblical Series, 11, ed. J. Reumann [Philadelphia: Fortress Press, 1964], p. 1-20). Discussions of the conception are numerous; cf. e.g., Best, *One Body*, pp. 203-207. Its most extended application to the study of Paul is R. P. Shedd, *Man in Community* (Grand Rapids: Eerdmans, 1964).
71. Cf. Tannehill, *Dying and Rising*, p. 5: "But 'corporate personality' is a phrase which covers up a lot of problems."
72. *Paul*, p. 64 (In the Dutch original [p. 63] the entire quote is italicized).
73. Ibid., p. 61: "On what this unity rests, whether it must be viewed, for example, as 'realistic' or as 'federal' is not further elucidated. At this point Ridderbos appears to be influenced by the exegesis of Berkouwer; cf. G. C. Berkouwer, *Sin*, trans. P. C. Holtrop (Grand Rapids: Eerdmans, 1971), pp. 511-532, see esp. p. 517.

relationship—the predestinarian and the redemptive-historical as well as the experiential. As we have already seen, the relation between the latter two aspects, particularly in view of their temporal distinctness, is difficult to grasp. But, if Paul describes the beginning of individual Christian existence in terms of resurrection with Christ, then we must presuppose for him the conception that God reckons and contemplates believers already as truly one with Christ at the time of his resurrection. "The mysteriousness of it must not be allowed to impair or tone down the reality of it in God's reckoning and in the actual constitution established by him in the union of his people with Christ."[74] While the distinctness of existential union may not be obscured, so too it needs to be emphasized that the scope of the corporate bond between Christ and believers is broader than the actual experience of the latter.

(2) Recognition must be given to the *primacy* or *constitutive* place of Christ in all aspects of this relationship. For Paul the union of Christ and believers involves more than the "identity of the individual and the group to which he belongs."[75] It is not a relationship of perfect reciprocity; nor is the direction of thought reversible. For instance, Paul neither says nor implies that Christ has been raised with believers.

(3) Recognition must be given to the *representative* significance of Christ in this relationship. This is perhaps most clear in II Corinthians 5:14f. Despite distinctive twists in phraseology and ideas, the orbit of thought is the same as in Romans 6:1ff. From the consideration that Christ died "for all," Paul directly draws the corporate conclusion that "all" died (v. 14).[76] Further, as in Romans 6 the purpose of

---

74. Murray, "Definitive Sanctification," p. 20. The words which immediately follow bear repeating here: "It is basic and central because only by virtue of what did happen in the past and finished historical does it come to pass in the sphere of the practical and existential that we actually come into possession of our identification with Christ when *he* died to sin and lived unto God."

75. H. W. Robinson, *Inspiration and Revelation in the Old Testament* (Oxford: Clarendon Press, 1946), p. 70. Robinson does recognize the prominence of certain individuals (Abraham, Noah, Moses) as representatives of the whole group (p. 82). Cf. Ridderbos, *Paul*, p. 33, n. 89: "In Paul it is not so much the representation of the whole by every part, as of the whole having been included in and being represented by a specific figure standing at the head."

76. Note the use of the conjunction "therefore" (ἄρα). Cf. L. S. Thornton, *The Common Life in the Body of Christ*, 3rd ed. (London: Dacre Press, 1950), p. 46: The words ("therefore all died") "refer, not simply to the consequences of the death of

death and burial with Christ is that believers might walk in newness of life (v. 4) and present "themselves to God" as "alive from the dead" (v. 13), so here the purpose of his death for all is that all might no longer live "for themselves" but "for him who died and was raised for them" (v. 15; cf. esp. Rom. 7:4). Paul never separates the corporate point of view from the representative. "ὑπέρ is not without σύν and σύν is not without ὑπέρ."[77]

Nevertheless, it is important to recognize that the two conceptions are distinct. The representative principle, the idea of the one *for* the many, not only reflects the primacy of Christ but also excludes a conception of corporate personality which obliterates the individuality of Christ.[78] The solidarity involved does not destroy the personal identity of either Christ or the believer. Accordingly, Paul's notion of Christ as a corporate person does *not* eliminate the necessity of reflecting on the place of an *ordo salutis* in Paul, on how he relates the benefits possessed (existentially and individually) by believers to the past historical accomplishment of Christ. In the language of classical theology, so far as the property of the believer in Christ is concerned, justice must be done both to the *alienum* and the *proprium,* and neither aspect may be stressed to the exclusion of the other.[79]

Summary and Conclusions

In this section we have examined Paul's teaching that believers have been raised with Christ. This teaching has a two-fold reference. It refers both to believers' involvement with Christ, their being reckoned one with Him at the time of his resurrection, and to the inception of individual Christian existence, the moment of being joined existentially to Christ. Thus this teaching involves the conception, so basic to Paul, of the union between Christ and believers. We examined this conception only, however, to the extent of iden-

Christ, but to something effected there and then, in and through the death upon the Cross. When Christ died something happened once for all, not only to him who died, but to all for whom he died. They also died with him upon the Cross."

77. Hahn, *Mitsterben und Mitauferstehen*, p. 147; cf. Ridderbos, *When the Time Had Fully Come*, pp. 53-57.

78. This is the error realized on a broad scale in the work of J. A. T. Robinson, *The Body. A Study in Pauline Theology*, SBT, 5 (London: SCM Press, 1953). Robinson finds in Paul a conception of the church according to which Christ becomes a suprapersonal entity.

79. Cf. J. Murray, *The Imputation of Adam's Sin* (Grand Rapids: Eerdmans, 1959), p. 88.

tifying several perspectives necessary to our subsequent investigation.

Beyond these summary observations, it will be useful here to draw two further conclusions of rather wide-ranging importance:

(1) Paul's teaching not only permits but demands the distinction between redemption accomplished and applied. As strongly as Paul stresses the organic bond between Christ's past historical experience and the present existence of the believer, he never obscures the definitive and completed character of the former. The distinction, however, may only be made in the light of the organic bond. Specifically, the solidaric tie between the realization of redemption in the life history of the believer and its past, definitive accomplishment is so strong and of such a nature that the former can only be understood and expressed in terms of the latter. The redemptive-historical perspective is both dominant and determinative. Further, because in Christ's resurrection the history of redemption has reached its eschatological consummation, the soteriological experience of the believer accordingly has an eschatological character. For Paul, eschatology is not only the goal of soteriology but also encompasses it, constituting its very substance from the outset.[80]

(2) The language of resurrection with which Paul describes the believer's entrance into a saved state is "not an occasional, figurative description of the experience, but obviously a piece of fixed doctrinal terminology."[81] "Raised with Christ" is not a general metaphorical usage subject to a theologically more precise delination, but a realistic description of the event that inaugurates individual Christian experience. It is a most basic element in Paul's soteriology; apart from it the structure of the whole cannot be grasped.

CONCLUSION

So far we have tried to show that the theme governing Paul's resurrection theology is the unity of the resurrec-

---

80. A suggestive development of this point is given by Vos, *Eschatology*, pp. 42-61; cf. for a formally similar emphasis, Schweitzer, *Mysticism*, pp. 138-140; also F. Guntermann, *Die Eschatologie des Hl. Paulus*, NA, 13 (Münster: Aschendorff, 1932), pp. 265-270.
81. Vos, *Eschatology*, p. 45.

tion of Jesus and the resurrection of believers. Jesus is raised in his specific identity as the second Adam. The first section dealt with the organic bond between Christ's resurrection and the future, bodily resurrection of the believer, and the second section with the connection between Christ's resurrection and the believer's experience of being joined to him existentially. Consequently, (1) *three* elements have to be considered: the resurrection of Jesus from the tomb, the initial soteric experience in the life history of the believer, and the future, bodily resurrection of the believer. (2) The organic tie between these elements has to be maintained.

Keeping these two structural guidelines in view, the unity of the resurrection of Christ and the resurrection of believers is such that the latter consists of two episodes in the experience of the individual believer—one which is past, already realized, and one which is future, yet to be realized. In the period between the resurrection and parousia of Christ, any believer is one who has already been raised from the dead, and is yet to be raised. The correspondence to the formal structure of Paul's eschatology at this point is not difficult to see. The distinctive notion that the eschaton, the "age-to-come," is both present and future,[82] is reflected in his teaching concerning the fundamental eschatological occurrence for the individual believer: his resurrection is both already and not yet.

Since these two aspects of the believer's experience are integrally related to each other as well as to the past event of Jesus' resurrection, the unity involved may be expressed by saying that the resurrection of Jesus is refracted in the experience of the believer in a two-fold fashion. This "refraction," however, does not obscure or eliminate the spatio-temporal distinctness of all three occurrences. The post-Kantian dualism of *Geschichte* and *Historie* is not found in Paul.

Is it possible to distinguish anthropologically the two aspects of the believer's experience of resurrection? The physical nature of the future resurrection would seem to

---

82. A still-classic treatment of the structure of Paul's eschatology, particularly his use of the doctrine of the two ages, is Vos, *Eschatology*, Chapter I, esp. pp. 36-41; cf. Kuss, *Römerbrief*, 289-291 and the literature cited there; H. Sasse, *TDNT*, 1:204-207.

furnish an obvious distinction. The difference could be expressed, then, in terms of non-bodily and bodily resurrection or a variety of similar contrasts: internal-external, invisible-visible, secret-open. For reasons to be noted below, the distinction "spiritual (=Holy Spirit)-physical (=bodily)" is definitely *not* acceptable. Perhaps best is a contrast suggested by Paul himself, namely, the contrast between "the inner man" (ὁ ἔσω ἄνθρωπος) and "the outer man" (ὁ ἔξω ἄνθρωπος), which occurs explicitly in II Corinthians 4:16. There the outer man is said to be decaying, while the inner man (cf. Rom. 7:22; Eph. 3:16) is being renewed daily. In the context, the decaying outer man corresponds to Paul's mortal flesh (v. 11) or, in view of the parallelism with verse 10, his body (cf. Rom. 6:12; 8:11). Similarly, the renewing of the inner man corresponds to the manifesting of the (resurrection) life of Jesus in Paul (vv. 10, 11). In effect, then, Paul is saying: the resurrection of the inner man is past; the resurrection of the outer man is still future (cf. v. 14).[83] This should not be understood, however, in the sense of an anthropological dualism.[84] Rather the dual aspect of the *whole* man is in view. Considered from the inward, hidden side of the believer, resurrection has taken place; from his outward, exposed side (including mental as well as physical faculties) resurrection is still outstanding. We can perhaps speak of the resurrection of the believer in the integral unity of his person as unfolding in two installments—one invisible, one visible.

The usage in Romans 7:22, while decidedly more ethical, does expand on the general contrast in terms of certain other, more specific anthropological categories. Here the inner man is closely associated with Paul's "mind" (νοῦς, v. 23) and contrasted with his "members" (μέλη, v. 23) and his body (v. 24). In Ephesians 3:16 the strengthening of the inner man is correlated with the indwelling of (the resurrected) Christ in the heart. Elsewhere "mind" and "heart" (καρδία) are closely associated (Phil. 4:7; II Cor. 3:14f.), while in Romans 12:2

---

83. Cf. Vos, *Eschatology*, p. 200.

84. Ridderbos (*Paul*, p. 155) comments concerning this distinction: "No general anthropological conclusions are to be drawn from this, however, e.g., of a dualistic man consisting of two 'parts,' or of a more or less 'real' or 'essential' part of man. Rather, the complete description—outward and inward 'man'—points in another direction; man does not only 'have' an outward and inward side, but is as man both 'outward' and 'inward,' exists both in the one way and in the other."; cf. P. Hughes, *Paul's Second Epistle to the Corinthians*, NICNT (Grand Rapids: Eerdmans, 1962), pp. 153-156.

the mind is the subject of renewal attributed to the inner man in II Corinthians 4:16. To sum up: so far as the believer is inner man, mind, and heart,[85] he has already been raised; so far as he is outer man, body, flesh ($\sigma\acute{\alpha}\rho\xi$ is synonymous with $\sigma\tilde{\omega}\mu\alpha$ in II Cor. 4:11, cf. v. 10; Gal. 4:13, 14), members, he is yet to be raised.[86]

THE ACTIVITY OF THE FATHER AND
THE PASSIVITY OF THE SON

The unity of the resurrection of Christ and the resurrection of the believer is confirmed in an indirect but massive fashion by those statements in which Paul refers to the simple fact of Jesus' resurrection. An examination of this material will also uncover still another fundamental element in his resurrection theology.[87]

In these expressions, forms of $\dot{\epsilon}\gamma\epsilon\acute{\iota}\rho\omega$ are most prominent, characteristically in the active voice (aorist) with Christ as object and God as subject (Rom. 10:9; I Cor. 6:14; 15:15; Acts 13:30, 37; cf. Eph. 2:6). Elsewhere Jesus is the object of the participial expression "he who raised," $\dot{\delta}$ $\dot{\epsilon}\gamma\epsilon\acute{\iota}\rho\alpha\varsigma$ (Rom. 4:24; 8:11; II Cor. 4:14; Col. 2:12). The aorist participle of $\dot{\alpha}\nu\acute{\iota}\sigma\tau\eta\mu\iota$ is similarly employed, modifying God, with Jesus as object (Acts 13:33; 17:31). On two occasions (Eph. 2:5; Col. 2:13) God is the subject and Christ an implied object of $\sigma\upsilon\nu\zeta\omega\sigma\pi\omega\iota\acute{\epsilon}\omega$ (aorist active).[88]

85. "that deepest and truest self" (Murray, *Romans*, 1:266); "the determinative 'center' of his actions" (Ridderbos, *Paul*, p. 118).
86. The close of this section is an appropriate place to touch on the question of the resurrection of unbelievers. Paul gives no indication of any positive *structural* relationship, much less unity, between it and the resurrection of Christ. He does, however, teach a "double" resurrection. This is most clear from the sermon before Felix (Acts 24:10-21). The "wicked" as well as the "righteous" are subjects of the coming resurrection (v. 15). Corroboratory evidence is the stress placed upon final judgment for all, both good and evil (Rom. 2:5-12, 16; II Cor. 5:10; II Thess. 1:8; cf. I Cor. 6:2; 11:32). In fact, however, Paul dwells almost exclusively on the "positive," i.e., the specifically soteric aspects of resurrection. H. A. A. Kennedy is basically correct when he says: "The question of a *general* resurrection lies outside of Paul's horizon, at least so far as definite discussions of the event are concerned" (*St. Paul's Conception of the Last Things*, 2nd ed. (London: Hodder and Stoughton, 1904), p. 275). The fullest treatment of this whole question is given by H. Molitor, *Die Auferstehung der Christen und Nichtchristen nach dem Apostel Paulus*, NA, 16 (Münster: Aschendorff, 1933); cf. Vos, *Eschatology*, pp. 215-225; Bultmann, *TDNT*, 3:17.
87. Whether or not these statements are pre-Pauline confessional or liturgical formulas need not be decided here. For the case for their pre-Pauline origin cf. esp. Kramer, *Christ, Lord, Son of God*, pp. 20ff.
88. Apparently no consideration deriving from the fact of resurrection or the state of being raised dictates Paul's choice of the object (or the subject when the verb is passive). All of the following occur: "Christ" (e.g., Rom. 6:4; I Cor. 15:15; Eph.

As to the subject "God" Paul can be more specific. He speaks of his own office of apostle, which he has "through Jesus Christ and God the Father, who raised him from the dead" (Gal. 1:1). In Ephesians 1 it is "the God of our Lord Jesus Christ, the Father of glory" (v. 17), who has worked in Christ, "raising him from the dead" (v. 20). He commends the Thessalonian Christians because they serve "the living and true God and wait for his Son from heaven, Jesus, whom he raised from the dead...." (I Thess. 1:9f.). In Romans 8:11 "he who raised," distinguished from both the Spirit and Jesus, is surely a reference to the Father. Finally, in Acts 13:33f. God raises Jesus in his identity as the Son of Psalm 2:7. It follows, then, that when Paul writes typically of Christ, "God raised him from the dead" (Rom. 10:9), he has in view the activity of the Father.[89]

This conclusion provides the background for understanding Paul's use of passive forms of ἐγείρω with Christ as subject. Approximately half of the occurrences of the verb are in this category (aorist passive: Rom. 4:25; 6:4, 9; 7:4; 8:34; II Cor. 5:15; perfect middle or passive: I Cor. 15:4, 12, 14, 16, 17, 20; II Tim. 2:8). Linguistically this usage is ambiguous, because in the New Testament passive forms of ἐγείρω in non-resurrection contexts are usually intransitive or, more accurately, they have active force (Matt. 1:24; 2:13; Mark 2:12; Luke 11:8; John 11:29; *et passim*; in Paul, Rom. 13:11 only). Where passive forms of the verb refer to Christ's resurrection, then, is their force intransitive-active or properly passive? In other words, is Paul in this usage reflecting on the agency of Jesus in his own resurrection?

The notion that Jesus is active in his resurrection, if present here, is not supported elsewhere in Paul. Rather, as already indicated, throughout stress is on the creative power and action of the Father of which Christ is the recipient (cf. Rom. 4:17). Vos, for one, is quite emphatic

89. Murray concludes with specific reference to the Pauline material, "There can, 1:20), "Jesus" (e.g., Rom. 8:11, I Thess. 1:10; Acts 13:33), "Lord" (I Cor. 6:14), "Christ Jesus" (Rom. 8:11[?], 34), "Jesus Christ" (Gal. 1:1; II Tim. 2:8), "Lord Jesus" (Rom. 10:9; II Cor. 4:14) and "Jesus our Lord" (Rom. 4:24).
then, be no question but that the Father as the first person of the Trinity is represented as the agent in the resurrection of Christ" ("Who Raised Up Jesus?", WTJ, 3 [1940-41]:114).

on this point: "Nowhere is it said of Jesus that He contributed towards his own resurrection, far less that He raised Himself."[90]

In fact, there is nothing in the verb itself that requires an intransitive-active meaning.[91] In I Corinthians 15:15, 32, 52, since the passive forms refer to the resurrection of believers, they can only have truly passive force. The usage in Colossians 2:12; 3:1 is particularly instructive in this respect. The verb (συνηγέρϑητε) has in view the resurrection of both Christ and believers, and so surely has the same passive force for the former that it necessarily has for the latter. In Philippians 2:9, Christ is the object of God's action described as "exalting highly" (ὑπερυψόω) and "giving" (χαρίζομαι), an action which, it will be argued below, includes the resurrection. Bengel's comment on verse 9 reflects our contention in this section: "Christ emptied Christ; God exalted Christ."[92]

In I Thessalonians 4:14 Paul writes: ". . . Jesus died and rose." Because second aorist forms of ἀνίστημι regularly have intransitive-active force (e.g. Mark 3:26; Luke 10:25; Acts 6:9), apparently Jesus' activity in his own resurrection is in view here. However, verse 16 adds that "the dead in Christ will rise (ἀναστήσονται) first." Similar to the verb usage in verse 14, the future middle of ἀνίστημι is always intransitive-active in its non-resurrection usage (Matt. 12:41; Luke 11:32; Acts 20:30). But this is plainly not its force here, where the resurrection of believers is in view, so that the intransitive use merely relates the action of rising to the subject without giving any indication of agency.[93] Hence, in view of

90. *Eschatology*, p. 147, n. 6; cf. D. H. Van Daalen, "The Resurrection of the Body and Justification by Grace," *Studia Evangelica*, ed. F. L. Cross, Texte und Untersuchuungen zur Geschichte der altchristlichen Literatur, 88 (Berlin: Akademie-Verlag, 1964), 3:219f.; A. Oepke, *TDNT*, 2:333ff.

91. Murray, who wishes to hold open the possibility that there may be a reflection on "Jesus' own agency" in its usage, nevertheless rightly maintains: "To *insist*, however, that there is reflection upon the agency of Christ in His own resurrection, in such usage as we have now been discussing, is not warranted" ("Who Raised Up Jesus?" p. 116).

92. J. A. Bengel, *New Testament Word Studies*, trans. C. T. Lewis and M. R. Vincent (Grand Rapids: Kregel Publications, 1971), 2:435. In view of the above observations the perfect of ἐγείρω used for the resurrection of Jesus (I Cor. 15:4, 12ff.; II Tim. 2:8) should be taken as a true passive rather than a middle. Cf. the emphasis placed on the activity of God (the Father) in I Cor. 15:15.

93. Note in the various English translations the use of the intransitive "rise" as the most natural rendering for passive forms of ἐγείρω even where the resurrection of others than Jesus is in view (cf., e.g., Matt. 9:25; Luke 7:14).

the close grammatical and contextual ties, the verb in verse 14, applied to Christ, has the same force.[94]

Conclusions. Two conclusions follow from this analysis of Paul's undeveloped references to Jesus' resurrection.[95] (1) God in his specific identity as the Father raises Jesus from the dead. This is a cardinal point, despite the tendency to lose sight of it in the course of more detailed exegetical work. (2) In his resurrection Jesus is viewed as entirely passive. It is, strictly speaking, not a rising but a being raised.[96]

The frequent yet offhand manner of Paul's references to Christ's passivity in his resurrection shows just how thoroughly his thinking is regulated by the unity of the resurrection of Christ and the resurrection of believers. In every instance Christ's passivity reflects his identity as "firstfruits" and "firstborn," his identification with "those who sleep," his solidarity with "the dead."

This uniform stress on passivity and solidarity with believers in the experience of resurrection points to the conclusion that the significance of Christ's resurrection does not lie where the difference between him and believers is most pronounced but in what they have in common. Paul is not primarily interested in Jesus' resurrection for its apologetic value as an especially evident display and powerful proof of his divinity. Rather, to anticipate major conclusions reached below, he views it as the vindication of the incarnate Christ in his sufferings and obedience unto death, as his constitution as "firstborn among many brothers" (Rom. 8:29). The resurrection of Christ is simply that—the resurrection of "the Christ," who in his experience is one with those on whose behalf

---

94. The expression ἀναστῆναι ἐκ νεκρῶν (Acts 17:3) should be understood in the light of the discussion in this paragraph. The only other instance in Paul where an intransitive of ἀνίστημι occurs (Eph. 5:14, second aorist imperative) involves the use of quoted (?) material of uncertain origin (cf. Grosheide, *Efeziërs*, pp. 82f.), addressed to believers.

95. In addition to Murray's article (cf. above, n. 89) helpful linguistic discussions are to be found in Vos, *Eschatology*, pp. 146f., n. 7 and Moliter, *Auferstehung*, pp. 13-16; cf. M. E. Dahl, *The Resurrection of the Body*, SBT, 36 (Naperville, Ill.: Alec R. Allenson, 1962), pp. 98-100.

96. The relationship of this emphasis to the statements of Jesus in John 2:19-22; 10:17, 18 must be passed over here. Murray (*Romans*, 1: 156) comments concerning Paul's stress on passivity: "This does no prejudice to the action of Jesus himself in his death and resurrection." Cf. "Who Raised Up Jesus?" pp. 118-123; C. Hodge, *A Commentary on the Epistle to the Romans*, p. 29.

he has been anointed. Or to express this solidaric, messianic factor in a broader, more distinctly Pauline category, it is the resurrection of the second Adam (I Cor. 15:22, 45). The resurrection of Jesus is just as thoroughly messianic and adamic as are his sufferings and death. His resurrection is as equally representative and vicarious as his death. Believers no longer live to themselves but to the Christ, "who for their sake died and was raised" (II Cor. 5:15).

THE AGENCY OF THE SPIRIT

Nothing is more basic to the structure of Paul's resurrection theology than the connection between the Holy Spirit and the resurrection of Christ. This conjunction is present in a variety of ways in passages to be looked at subsequently. Here we limit ourselves to considering the Spirit's *instrumentality* in the resurrection of Jesus.

Romans 8:11

While Paul nowhere says explicitly that Jesus was raised by the Spirit, this is his clear presupposition. In Romans 8:9-11, against the background of the antithesis between "flesh" and Spirit discussed in the chapter's opening verses, Paul notes some implications of the Spirit's dwelling in believers. The assumption expressed in verse 9a ("if the Spirit of God dwells in you") is basic to the reasoning in the sentences immediately following. Essential also is the intimate bond between Christ and the Spirit. The Spirit is the "the Spirit of Christ" (v. 9b). In the experience of believers, "in the Spirit" (v. 9a), "the Spirit in you" (vv. 9a, 11a, c) and "Christ in you" (v. 10a) are all used correlatively, and the remaining possibility on this combination, the more usual "in Christ," is certainly present by implication (cf. the apodosis of v. 9b; v. 1). The idea of solidarity, then, has an important place in these verses.

From these considerations Paul draws two implications, one regarding the believer's present (v. 10b) and the other regarding his future (v. 11). The latter concerns us here. The central thought in verse 11 is that God will make alive the mortal bodies of believers "through his Spirit, who dwells in you."[97] This, it should be noted,

97. Even if the variant, διά with the accusative, is adopted, the idea of the Spirit's activity is still suggested and difficult to eliminate. Cf. Murray, *Romans*, 1:292, n. 14.

forms the conclusion to an argument. Rather diffusely, it may at first seem, the indwelling Spirit is described as "the Spirit of him who raised Jesus from the dead" (v. 11a), and the one who will enliven believers through the indwelling Spirit (the Father) is described as "He who raised Christ Jesus from the dead" (v. 11b).

This doubly underscored reference to the Father as the one who raised Jesus from the dead shows Paul to be reasoning on the basis of the analogy between Christ and believers in the experience of resurrection: what the Father has done for the one he will also do for the others.[98] This analogy, in turn, reflects the solidarity, emphasized in the immediate context, which is so basic for Paul, particularly in relation to the resurrection: what is true for the "firstfruits" holds for the rest of the harvest.

The references to the indwelling Spirit in verse 11, then, strengthen the basic line of reasoning by analogy. Hence the thought is that the instrument employed by the Father in the resurrection of Jesus (and which he will also employ in the future resurrection of believers) is already at work in them. In other words, the implication is that the Spirit worked instrumentally in the resurrection of Christ.[99] If this were not the case, bringing in Christ's resurrection in connection with the indwelling Spirit in the argument of verse 11 would have no point.

Romans 8:11 also discloses why the distinction "spiritual-physical"[100] is inadequate for distinguishing the present (past) and future aspects of resurrection in the believer's experience. To be sure, the realized aspect is decidedly spiritual. In this context verse 10 makes it clear that the present life of the believer is the Spirit.[101] But as verse 11 reveals, the spiritual qualification of the future resurrection is no less definite. In fact, the single adjec-

---

98. For the argument in this paragraph cf. esp. Vos, *Eschatology*, pp. 163f.

99. Thus the thought of the Spirit's activity (in Jesus' resurrection) is present entirely apart from the question of the textual variant; see above, n. 97.

100. So, e.g., Murray, *Romans*, 1:218 (on 6:5): "The apostle is not dealing here with our physical death and resurrection; he is dealing with our death to sin and our resurrection to Spiritual life. . . ."

101. In contrast to the almost universal older consensus, recent interpretation has recognized increasingly that πνεῦμα (v. 10) is not anthropological but a reference to the Holy Spirit; so, e.g., Murray, *Romans*, 1:289-291; Ridderbos, *Romeinen*, p. 177; O. Michel, *Der Brief an die Römer*, MeyerK, 4, 11th ed. (Göttingen: Vandenhoeck & Ruprecht, 1957), pp. 163f.

tive chosen by Paul to describe the future resurrection body both comprehensively and distinctively is
"spiritual" (I Cor. 15:44). The somatic aspect of resurrection, even more than what has already been experienced,
will disclose the full dimensions of the Holy Spirit's work
in the believer.

The Spirit, Power, Glory, and Life

According to Paul, Christ has been raised "through the
glory of the Father" (Rom. 6:4), "through his power"
(I Cor. 6:14),[102] "according to the working of the strength
of his might" (Eph. 1:19; cf. Col. 2:12). Having been
crucified because of weakness, he lives "by God's power" (II
Cor. 13:4). His being declared Son of God in power by the
resurrection of the dead is "according to the Spirit of
holiness" (Rom. 1:4).

Only the last of these expressions explicitly mentions
the Spirit. However, exploring the pattern of word associations which ties them together will disclose that his activity is in view in each one, as well as other aspects of
Paul's pneumatology pertinent to this study.

The close connection between the Spirit and glory
(δόξα) is not difficult to recognize. The "spiritual body" of
the believer is raised "in glory" (I Cor. 15:43f.).
Analogously, the body of the resurrected Christ, the
"life-giving Spirit" (I Cor. 15:45) is the "body of his
glory" (Phil. 3:21). The ministry of the Spirit is a ministry
"in glory" *par excellence* (II Cor. 3:8; cf. "the surpassing
glory" (v. 10). As believers behold "the glory of the
Lord," who is "the Spirit," they are transformed into his
image "from glory to glory," and this "as from the Lord,
the Spirit" (II Cor. 3:17f.; cf. 4:4, 6). In the parallelism of
I Timothy 3:16 Christ's justification "in the Spirit" is correlated with his ascension "in glory."

---

102. The antecedent of "his" is "God" and the phrase probably modifies the first
verb in the verse as well. Against Grosheide (*I Cor.*, p. 148), who refers the phrase
to the second verb only and the possessive to "Lord." This gives the idea that God
raises the Lord and then raises believers through his (the Lord's) power. Syntactically, this is possible but not most natural; cf. Weiss, *I Korintherbrief*, p. 162; A.
Robertson and A. Plummer, *A Critical and Exegetical Commentary on the First Epistle of
St. Paul to the Corinthians*, ICC, 2nd ed. (New York: Scribner's, 1929), p. 124.
Theologically, although certainly not un-Pauline, it reflects a failure to appreciate sufficiently the fundamental elements of Paul's resurrection theology (cf. here esp. Rom.
8:11; II Cor. 4:14).

If anything, the association of the Spirit with power (δύναμις) is even more intimate.[103] Paul's preaching at Thessalonica was "in power and in the Holy Spirit" (I Thess. 1:5), at Corinth "in the demonstration of the Spirit and power" (I Cor. 2:4). A close correlation is evident in each of these phrases, especially in the latter. The underlying thought is: "Where spirit is, there is power, and where power is, spirit."[104] This virtual synonymity explains why in I Corinthians 2:5—where the purpose of the immediate and broader context (cf. vv. 10-16) is to stress the spiritual qualification necessary for understanding the gospel—Paul can simply say that his listeners' (Spirit-worked) faith is grounded "in God's power." Elsewhere Paul prays that the Roman Christians may abound in hope "by the power of the Holy Spirit" (Rom. 15:13), and glories that Christ works through him "in the Spirit's power" (v. 19). The declaration of Jesus as Son of God "in power" is "according to the Spirit" (Rom. 1:4), and the "spiritual body" is raised "in power" (I Cor. 15:43f.). Romans 8:11 and I Corinthians 6:14, then, express the same thought in relation to Christ's resurrection. The agency the former verse attributes to the Spirit is ascribed to power in the latter.[105]

The various expressions used to indicate agency in Jesus' resurrection are explained by the correlation among the Spirit, power, and glory which permits them to be used interchangeably. "Life" (ζωή) too is in this group.[106] In fact, these four notions together constitute a rather tightly-knit conceptual complex. Each has its own broader associations, but the intimate ties existing among them are especially pronounced. These lines of affinity are further confirmed by the close connections between glory and power (I Cor. 15:43, Eph. 1:18; 3:16; Col. 1:11; II Thess. 1:9), glory and life (Rom. 2:7; I Cor. 15:43; Col. 3:4), and power and life (I Cor. 15:54; II Cor. 13:4). Also,

103. The various words for power used by Paul may be treated here as synonyms; cf. Grosheide, *Efeziërs*, p. 30, n. 48; O. Schmidt, "Der Begriff ΔΥΝΑΜΙΣ bei Paulus," *Festgabe für Adolf Deissmann* (Tübingen: J. C. B. Mohr, 1927), p. 164.
104. E. Sokolowski, *Die Begriffe Geist und Leben bei Paulus* (Göttingen: Vandenhoeck & Ruprecht, 1903), p. 2.
105. For further discussion of the Spirit-power relationship in Paul, cf. Sokolowski, *Begriffe*, pp. 1-4; W. Grundmann, *Der Begriff der Kraft in der neutestamentlichen Gedankenwelt* (Stuttgart: W. Kohlhammer, 1932), pp. 97-106.
106. The intimate bond between Spirit and life is apparent in Rom. 8:2, 6, 10; I Cor. 15:45; II Cor. 3:6; cf. Gal. 5:25; 6:8; Rom. 6:4 with 7:6.

when the fundamental antithesis between "flesh" and the Spirit (e.g. Rom. 8:4ff.; Gal. 3:3; 5:16; Phil. 3:3) is in view, then "weakness," repeatedly the counterpart of power, is not only closely associated with "flesh" but sharply contrasted with the Spirit (Rom. 6:19; 8:3, 26; 15:1; I Cor. 2:3f.; 3:3; 15:43; II Cor. 10:4; 12:9; 13:3f.; Gal. 4:13). The close interrelations within this conceptual network are perhaps most clear in I Corinthians 15:42ff.: the resurrection body described as "spiritual," whose primary exemplification is Christ as "life-giving Spirit," will be raised "in immortality" (cf. Rom. 2:7; II Tim. 1:10), "glory," and "power."

So far as relations within this conceptual complex are concerned, priority clearly belongs to the Spirit. Life, power, and glory on the one hand, and the Spirit on the other, are related as "products to the Producer."[107] The Spirit enjoys the precedence which belongs to a personal agent in distinction from his functions. At the same time, however, it is true that the "main peculiarity [in Paul's teaching on the Spirit] consists in the enveloping, circumambient, one might also say atmospheric character of the Spirit's working, a feature first clearly emerging with Paul, and that so strongly as to give at times almost the impression as though the personal character of the Spirit's mode of existence were obscured by it."[108] This nonpersonal air is present where Paul substitutes glory or power for the Spirit as the instrument employed in the resurrection of Christ and the believer, as well as in the broader synonymous interchange of Spirit and power. A similar elemental or atmospheric conception plays an important role in several of the passages to be examined below.[109]

The Person of the Spirit

Not surprisingly, then, a significant segment of recent interpretation has concluded that Paul does not view the Spirit as a person. Ernst Käsemann states: "For Paul the

---

107. Vos, *Eschatology*, p. 302. Vos gives perhaps the most penetrating treatment of this relationship (pp. 302-315). His conclusion is that life and power are related to the inner, hidden side, and glory to the outer side of the eschatological transformation wrought by the Spirit (p. 314).

108. Vos, *Eschatology*, p. 59; cf. pp. 163, 165f.

109. An impersonal tone is especially pronounced in I Cor. 12:13, Eph. 1:13, and I Thess. 5:19.

divine spirit is a power, indeed a miraculous power, which from the viewpoint of the history of religions is classified with the concept of 'Mana.' Thus for Paul spirit and power are correlate ideas." More particularly, Käsemann says the Spirit is "thought of materially and substantially."[110] Bultmann thinks that in an unreflecting way Paul has been influenced by various traditional (for the most part, hellenistic) views of the Spirit.[111] None of these views represents Paul's real intention; but among them is the conception of πνεῦμα as "a non-worldly material."[112] "In dynamistic thinking . . . πνεῦμα appears as an impersonal force which fills man like a fluid, so to say."[113] The Roman Catholic scholar, Ingo Hermann, although wishing to avoid every "reification" (*Verdinglichung*) of the Spirit, nevertheless feels that Paul's language "prohibits for an interpretation of Paul every hypostatization of the spirit in the direction of an independent third person of the Trinity. . . ." And Hermann concludes: "Paul does not think of the spirit as a person, certainly, however, as personal in the sense of a power radiating from the divine being and activity, and permeated by the personality of God or Christ."[114]

In my judgment, however, even a brief survey of the material shows clearly that Paul considers the Spirit a (divine) person in the same sense as the Father and Christ.[115] While the thought of Galatians 4:6 is obviously close to Romans 8:15, it is not precisely the same. The crying attributed to believers in Romans 8:15 is in Galatians 4:6 the (personal) activity of the Spirit himself. Nothing permits, much less requires, toning down the force of Galatians 4:6. The cry is his, not theirs, and

---

110. *Leib und Leib Christi*, Beiträge zur historischen Theologie, 9 (Tübingen: J. C. B. Mohr, 1933), p. 125.
111. For a development of this theory cf. E. Schweizer, *TDNT*, 6:415-424.
112. *Theology*, 1:333 (Bultmann's italics).
113. Ibid., p. 155.
114. *Kyrios und Pneuma*, pp. 140f.; cf. pp. 57f.
115. Concerning Paul's conception of God, Warfield's assessment seems most accurate: "We shall not say that there are the beginnings of the doctrine of the Trinity here. It seems truer to say that there is the clear presupposition of some such doctrine as that of the Trinity here" (*The Lord of Glory* [Grand Rapids: Zondervan, n.d.], p. 229). Cf. H. Bertrams, *Das Wesen des Geistes nach der Anschauung des Apostels Paulus*, NA, 4 (Münster: Aschendorff, 1913), p. 170.

belongs with the "joint-witness" (συμμαρτυρεῖν) ascribed to him in Romans 8:16.

In Romans 8:26f. the assistance of the Spirit is not an indwelling power which offsets the weakness of believers and enables them to pray as they should (καθὸ δεῖ). It is, rather, an intercessory activity of the Spirit which does not have an activity of believers as a component or even a counterpart. The groaning is his, not theirs. His intercession is not theirs but on behalf of them. Verse 27b stresses this by saying that he intercedes "for the saints." In the immediate context (v. 34), a parallel activity of intercession is ascribed to Christ (with the same verb used of the Spirit in v. 27).

The admonition against grieving the Holy Spirit in Ephesians 4:30 has as its obvious presupposition that the Spirit is capable of emotional life.

It is difficult to avoid the conclusion that in Romans 15:30 and I Corinthians 6:11, where Christ and the Spirit are correlated instrumentally, the Spirit is viewed as a person, standing on a line with Christ.[116] The reference is not simply to a display of power or the mode of Christ's working.

I Corinthians 12:4ff., II Corinthians 13:13, and Ephesians 4:4ff. have a common triadic structure: the (Holy) Spirit is correlated with God (the Father) and the Lord (Jesus Christ). To maintain that the Spirit is not in view as a person but refers to God's powerful activity destroys the parallel. No doubt both I Corinthians 12 and Ephesians 4 have in view the activity of God. But this work is surveyed by focusing attention on the distribution of functions among the Father, Christ, and the Spirit. Plainly the Spirit is placed on the side of the divine persons as distinct from all divine workings, activities, and functions. In II Corinthians 13:13 elimination of a reference to the person of the Spirit inevitably involves recourse to the syntactically intolerable expedient of rendering the third genitive ("the fellowship of the Holy Spirit") differently than the first two. By analogy it is a

---

116. In Romans 15:30 πνεύματος is subjective genitive, cf. Murray, *Romans*, 2:221.

subjective genitive and points unmistakably to the Spirit as a person.[117]

How does the conclusion that the Spirit is a (divine) person relate to the nonpersonal modes of expression already noted? Does Paul's teaching on the Spirit contain two unconnected and irreconcilable conceptions?[118] Ephesians 4:30 shows how naturally and closely he associates these two elements: *because* it is he with whom they were sealed, believers are not to grieve the Spirit. Perhaps Paul's christological teaching provides a parallel which helps to make his pneumatological outlook clear. Occasionally, Christ can be referred to in nonpersonal terms; he is power and wisdom (I Cor. 1:24; cf. 30). Again, nothing is more personal than the relationship between Christ and believers. Yet this fellowship is based on their being "in Christ," a phrase which suggests that Christ is viewed atmospherically rather than personally. This characteristic expression is not felt to create a fundamental disjunction in Paul's christology, nor does it obliterate the personality of Christ; thus the presence of both personal and nonpersonal elements in his teaching on the Spirit need not be considered an incongruity.[119] This analogical consideration is given added weight by Paul's use of "in Christ" which over a large part of its range of application parallels "in the Spirit" in such a fashion that the two phrases are equivalent (cf. esp. Rom. 8:9-11).

117. For an extensive defense of the personality of the Spirit in Paul cf. esp. K. Stalder, *Das Werk des Geistes in der Heiligung bei Paulus* (Zürich: EVZ Verlag, 1962), pp. 19-69. Cf. J. Schildenberger ("2 Kor 3,17a: 'Der Herr aber ist der Geist' im Zusammenhang des Textes und der Theologie des Hl. Paulus," *Analecta Biblica*, 17:459): "The deity of the Spirit stands out clearly in the New Testament; however, because he appears as Spirit of God and of Christ, and as power and imparted gift, his personality stands out less clearly; he has, as it were, no face. Conversely, the personality of the Son appears clearly beside that of the Father, but his deity stands out less clearly. Still, both the personality of the Spirit as well as the identity in substance of the nature of the Son with the Father are clearly enough attested in the New Testament."

118. The view, e.g., of Bultmann, *Theology*, 1:155ff.; Schweizer, *TDNT*, 6:415ff.

119. Cf. Vos, *Eschatology*, p. 166: "If to be 'in Christ,' and at the same time to live in conscious intercourse and fellowship with Him are not logically identical, and are yet to our common Christian faith joined in the same believing subject without endangering the recognition of the one aspect by that of the other, then why should an analogous double relationship of the Holy Spirit to our persons be deemed incongruous?"; W. D. Davies, *Paul and Rabbinic Judaism. Some Rabbinic Elements in Pauline Theology* (New York: Harper & Row, 1967), pp. 182f.

CONCLUSION

Paul's teaching on the resurrection has a trinitarian character. Although never stated in so many words, the fundamental thought is that God the Father has raised up the Son through the Spirit.[120] All three persons have a direct interest and involvement. This consideration together with a second, namely, that the Son is raised in his specific identity as the second Adam, provides the matrix for all further theological reflection by the apostle.

120. Cf. Koch, "L'aspect eschatologique," p. 138: "For Saint Paul it is always God the Father who has raised Jesus through the Spirit."

PART THREE

*THE RESURRECTION OF
CHRIST IN PAUL'S
SOTERIOLOGY:*

The Development of the Theme

I N PART III OUR INTEREST is in the development Paul gives to the central theme identified along with its primary structural elements in Part II. However, the various aspects of his teaching are so thoroughly structured and interrelated that an "ideally" comprehensive treatment of this development would be tantamount to writing a definitive Pauline theology. Consequently, necessary bounds to the present discussion will be set by making use of the set of issues raised in the introduction. These may be reduced here to one question: How does Paul relate the resurrection of Jesus to the realization of redemption in the life history of the individual believer? Or, more generally, what for Paul is the relationship between the history of redemption and the *ordo salutis* (the *heilshistorisch* and the *heilsordelijk*), between the accomplishment and application of redemption?

An answer to this question, already broadly indicated, particularly in Part II, will now be worked out in detail by exploring precisely how Paul associates the resurrection with the central soteriological categories of justification, adoption, sanctification and glorification. In keeping with the controlling motif of the resurrection-unity between Christ and believers, we will first examine the theological significance of the experience of resurrection for Christ himself in his identity as the Messiah and second Adam (first section), and then how this teaching is related to the application of redemption, particularly the notion of being raised with Christ (second section).[1]

1. On the principal passages discussed in the first section, cf. esp. J. P. Versteeg, *Christus en de Geest . . . volgens de brieven van Paulus* (Kampen: J. H. Kok, 1971), who reaches the same basic conclusions, particularly on the relationship between the exalted Christ and the Spirit. I hope elsewhere to take up the diverging conclusions of J. D. G. Dunn ("II Corinthians 3:17—'The Lord is the Spirit,' "*Journal of Theological Studies*, New Series, 21(1970):309-320; "Jesus—Flesh and Spirit: an Exposition of Romans 1:3-4," *Journal of Theological Studies*, New Series, 24(1973):40-68; "I Corinthians 15:45—Last Adam, Life-giving Spirit," in ed. B. Lindars and S. S. Smalley, *Christ and Spirit in the New Testament: Studies in Honour of C. F. D. Moule* (Cambridge: University Press, 1973), pp. 127-141).

THE RESURRECTION OF CHRIST

I Corinthians 15:45

Our interest in this verse is the description of Christ, the last Adam, as "lifegiving *pneuma*" ($\pi\nu\epsilon\hat{\upsilon}\mu\alpha$ $\zeta\omega\sigma\pi\omega\hat{\upsilon}\nu$). However, nowhere in the whole of Paul is a statement more inextricably embedded in both its narrower and broader contexts. In verses 45-49 together with verse 22, "Paul provides us with what is one of the most striking and significant rubrics in all of Scripture."[2] Compact modes of expression and the density of thought also make it, along with verses 42-44, one of the most difficult. Some consideration, then, needs to be given to this contextual factor.

In verse 35 Paul takes up the questions of the mode of the resurrection and the nature of the resurrection body. These questions appear to have been posed by the opponents,[3] probably in a derisive fashion.[4] Paul, however, treats them seriously, making of them a single, compound question which structures his discussion to the end of the chapter. Within this section, the unit of verses 42-49 contains the heart of the argument.

An essential mark of this unit is its carefully implemented antithetical structure. The semantic function of particular clauses or phrases or even words is decisively controlled by their place in the central contrast running through verses 42-49. All too frequently the history of interpretation has failed to recognize this. Remembering, then, that our final objective is not the solution of all exegetical difficulties but the explanation of verse 45c, what are the central features in the development of the argument?

The contrast as begun in verses 42f. is between the dead body of the believer and his resurrection body.

---

2. Murray, *The Imputation of Adam's Sin*, p. 39.

3. Rather than a flat denial of the future, bodily resurrection of believers the Corinthian heresy may well have been a gnostically motivated "spiritualization" based on a one-sided appeal to Paul's own teaching in Rom. 6:3ff.; Eph. 2:5f.; Col. 2:12f., and similar to the error of Hymenaeus and Philetus ("the resurrection has already taken place," II Tim. 2:17f.); cf. H. Ridderbos, *De pastorale Brieven*, CNT (Kampen: J. H. Kok, 1967), p. 211; J. Jeremias, *Die Briefe an Timotheus und Titus*, NTD, 9 (Göttingen: Vandenhoeck & Ruprecht, 1963), p. 50.

4. "Fool!" (v. 36) indicates the sharpness of Paul's reply.

Although, strictly speaking, the corpse of the believer is in view (the four-fold repetition of "it is sown" [σπείρεται] makes this clear), implicitly present as well is the somatic condition of the believer prior to physical death. For Paul elsewhere refers believers to their mortal bodies (Rom. 6:12, 8:10f.; II Cor. 4:10f.; cf. here esp. vv. 53f.) and speaks of his own body at the time of writing as a "body of death" (Rom. 7:24). Even at the outset, then, the scope of the contrast is broadened by implication. At any rate, the one body is characterized by perishability, dishonor, and weakness, the other by imperishability, glory, and power. The prepositional phrases indicate circumstances or qualities of the subject rather than the manner in which the action of the verb takes place.[5] Even at these subordinate points of contrast the balanced, antithetical parallelism is carefully maintained.

Verse 44a summarizes what precedes. The single terms used to describe in a comprehensive and distinguishing fashion the bodies being contrasted are "natural," "psychical" (ψυχικόν) and "spiritual," respectively.

Careful attention to grammar discloses an important turn in the argument at verse 44b. The contrast up to this point carried out by a series of contraposed main clauses is continued by joining an apodosis to a protasis ("If there is a psychical body, there is also a spiritual body"). In other words, verse 44b is itself an *argument*. Without destroying the balanced parallelism, the rigid and pointed antithesis of verses 42-44a is suddenly softened. Paul now reasons directly from the psychical body to the spiritual body. The former is made the condition for the latter; the latter is postulated on the basis of the former.

Verse 45 supports verse 44b by an appeal to Scripture. "Thus it is written" makes this clear.[6] The particular use of Scripture is itself one of the striking features of this verse, for Paul in citing Genesis 2:7 which mentions only the creation of (the first) Adam, finds there also a

---

5. Grosheide, *I Corinthians*, pp. 384f.
6. So the nearly universal consensus of the commentaries (although the appeal itself has been given a number of differing evaluations). Grosheide's failure to see this point (which significantly mars his understanding of the passage as a whole) is difficult to explain (*I Cor.*, p. 386). It is true, as he points out, that verse 45 provides an additional thought, but this does not prohibit it from grounding the argument of verse 44b.

reference to the becoming of the last Adam. Two considerations show this: (1) Verse 45 functions to establish the *argument* in verse 44b. This it can do only as the appeal to Scripture covers the entire proposition, not just the protasis. (2) The syntax of verse 45 shows the close bond between 45b and 45c. The two clauses are joined asyndetically, their respective structures are closely parallel, and "become" (ἐγένετο, from the quotation) in the former is plainly to be read in the latter.[7]

How Paul arrived at this formulation is difficult to say. Although a certain similarity exists with the paraphrases of the Targums,[8] there is no evidence of borrowing. Original with him,[9] it is best understood as an annotation of Scripture equated with Scripture itself.[10]

As verse 45 grounds the argument of verse 44b, then, the references to the first Adam as "living soul" (ψυχὴ ζῶσα) and the last Adam (Christ) as "life-giving *pneuma*" (πνεῦμα ζωοποιοῦν) serve to establish a frame of reference for understanding "psychical" (ψυχικόν) and "spiritual" (πνευματικόν), respectively. Whatever else may be in view, the two are representatives or primary exemplifications. Adam is ὁ ψυχικός, Christ ὁ πνευματικός *par excellence*.

The trend of Paul's argument and his broadened perspectives on the resurrection of the body now begin to emerge. The contrast initiated between bodies has been expanded to include whole, living persons, persons who represent others. Moreover, on the one side, where the corpse of the believer was the point of departure, the scope has been expanded to include the person of Adam by virtue of *creation*.

Recognizing this expansion facilitates understanding verse 44b as an argument. At first glance, Paul's reasoning

---

7. Cf. P. Bachmann, *Der erste Brief des Paulus an die Korinther*, ZahnK, 7, 3rd ed. (Leipzig: A. Deichert, 1921), p. 466: "In view of οὕτως the scriptural proof would only be an incomplete attempt, if the second and really decisive element ὁ ἔσχατος . . . πνεῦμα ζωοποιοῦν were not also intended as a constituent part of the proof; only so also was the close syntactical tie between this and the preceeding clause possible."
8. Cf. Weiss, *I. Korintherbrief*, p. 373.
9. This is the interpretative consensus at present. Cf. R. Scroggs, *The Last Adam. A Study in Pauline Anthropology* (Philadelphia: Fortress Press, 1966), p. 86.
10. Note that already in verse 45b the text of Genesis 2:7 has been modified with the insertions of "first" and "Adam." E. E. Ellis, among others, sees in this and the verse as a whole an instance of *pesher* quotation (*Paul's Use of the Old Testament* (Edinburgh: Oliver and Boyd, 1957), pp. 143f.).

is apparently *a fortiori*: if there is a psychical body characterized by corruption, dishonor, weakness, then all the
more must there be a spiritual—powerful, glorified, incorruptible—body.[11] A major difficulty with this view, however, is that death and the qualities of the psychical body
in verses 42f. are for Paul always the result of sin (Rom.
5:12; 6:16, 21, 23; cf. Rom. 1:32; 8:6, 13; I Cor. 15:56; Gal.
6:8); and when he argues *a fortiori* from sin and condemnation to grace and salvation the form he regularly
employs is: "if ... much more. ..." ($\epsilon\iota$ ... $\pi o\lambda\lambda\tilde{\omega}$ $\mu\tilde{a}\lambda\lambda ov$
..., Rom. 5:15, 17; cf. II Cor. 3:7f., 9, 11). Moreover, ap-
parently all *a fortiori* arguments in Paul involving a
protasis with $\epsilon\iota$ have this form (or its equivalent) in the
apodosis (cf. Rom. 5:10; 11:12). Paul's usage elsewhere,
then, favors taking verse 44b as not containing a disquali-
fying element in the protasis and reasoning *directly* from
the psychical body to the spiritual body.

This conclusion, however, is apparently faced with an
insuperable difficulty of its own. How can Paul say that
the resurrection body with its attributes may be
predicated on the basis of the body placed in the tomb
with its attributes? Is Paul saying that death and life are
so related synthetically that the latter can be directly inferred from the former? Such a notion is in flat contracition
with Paul's uniform teaching elsewhere. Romans 5:12-21
demonstrates clearly that life and death are no more capable of being positively correlated and postulated from
each other than are righteousness and sin (cf. Rom. 6:20-
23; 8:2, 6; II Cor. 2:15f.).

A way out of this dilemma, which at the same time does
justice to the requirements of the text, is to recognize that
"psychical" in verse 44b has a significantly broader
reference than in verse 44a. The psychical body of verse
44b is the prefall, creation body, to which the characteristics (corruption, dishonor, weakness) of the psychical
body of verse 44a do not belong.[12] This inference is sup-

---

11. Where attention is paid to verse 44b as an argument, this in some form is the
explanation almost always given; so Grosheide, *I Cor.*, p. 385; Bachmann, *I. Kor.*,
p. 466; Charles Hodge, *An Exposition of the First Epistle to the Corinthians* (Grand
Rapids: Eerdmans, 1956), p. 348.
12. It will not do, while recognizing that the creation body is in view in verse 44b,
to extend to it the depreciatory predicates of verses 42f. Paul teaches too plainly
elsewhere (Rom. 5:12ff.) that these things result not from Adam's creation but from
his disobedience. Cf. Althaus, *Der Brief an die Römer*, p. 88.

ported by Paul's appeal in verse 45 to the creation of
Adam. In fact, these two factors—the argument of verse
44b and the use of Genesis 2:7 in verse 45—together en-
force the view that the psychical body of verse 44b is the
prefall body.[13]

Why does Paul, when asked about the nature of the
resurrection body and after beginning to contrast the
believer's dead body with his resurrection body, suddenly expand the comparison to include the creation
body? Apparently his interest is to show that from the
beginning, prior to the fall, a higher or different kind of
body than the body of Adam, the psychical body, is in
view. Adam, by virtue of creation (not because of sin), an-
ticipates and points to another, higher form of somatic existence. The principle of typology enunciated in Romans
5:14 is present here, albeit somewhat differently: the
creation body of Adam is "a type of the one to come." This
suggestion of typology helps to illumine the use of
Genesis 2:7 in verse 45, especially the addition in 45c.[14]

If at verse 45 the contrast has been expanded to include
the persons of Adam (prior to the fall) and Christ as representative of others, then its scope is really even broader;

13. Grosheide's argument (*I Cor.*, p. 386) that not man in general but Adam as an
individual is in view in verse 45, besides missing the connection with verse 44b, fails
to do justice to the fact that Paul always treats Adam (and Christ) as corporate, representative persons.
14. This is the position of Vos (*Eschatology*, pp. 169f., n. 19) which appears to be
unique with him: "The proper solution seems to be as follows: the Apostle was intent upon showing that in the plan of God from the outset provision was made for a
higher kind of body (as pertaining to a higher state of existence generally). From the
abnormal body of sin no inference could be drawn to that effect. The abnormal and
the eschatological are not so logically correlated that the one can be postulated from
the other. But the world of creation and the world to come *are* thus correlated, the
one pointing forward to the other; on the principle of typology the first Adam
prefigures the last Adam, the psychical body the pneumatic body (cp. Rom. v.
14). . . . The quotation proves this, because the 'psychical' as such is typical of the
pneumatic, the first creation of the second, the world that now is (if conceived
without sin) of the aeon to come." Identical views are expressed much earlier in "Eschatology and the Spirit," p. 232, n. 28.
  This correlation of protology and eschatology does not necessitate attributing to
Paul the notions that creation is inherently in need of redemption or that the works
of creation and redemption are identical. These are plainly excluded by what he
says in these verses and elsewhere. What this passage does teach is that the eschatological prospect held out to Adam (and which he failed to attain) is realized and
receives its specific character *de facto* by the work of the last Adam. The following
three propositions define the limits of further dogmatic reflection on these verses: (1)
Eschatology is a postulate of protology. (2) Soteriology is *not* a postulate of
protology. (3) Soteriology is eschatology.

it includes the environments of which Adam and Christ in their respective (bodily) existences are necessarily exponential. That Paul actually introduces such an extended horizon emerges in verse 46. Whatever may be the reason that Paul here momentarily departs from his parallel structure,[15] the contrast is not blunted but continued in significantly more general terms, and "psychical" and "spiritual" now describe two comprehensive states of affairs, two orders of existence contrasted temporally. The one follows upon the other and together they encompass the whole of history. Verse 46 is a compressed overview of history. As the era of the first Adam, the psychical order is the preeschatological aeon, the incomplete, transitory, and provisional world-age. As the era of the last Adam, the pneumatic order is the eschatological aeon, the complete, definitive, and final world-age. "τὸ πνευματικόν and τὸ ψυχικόν in verse 46 are generalizing expressions, after which it would be a mistake to supply σῶμα; they designate the successive reign of two comprehensive principles in history, two successive world-orders, a first and a second creation, beginning each with an Adam of its own."[16] The perspective from which Paul views the believer's resurrection, then, is nothing less than cosmic.

While verses 47-49 resume the balanced, antithetical parallelism, the contrast, up to this point expressed by ψυχή and πνεῦμα, with their adjectives, is continued by the pair "earth-heaven" (γῆ-οὐρανός) and related adjectives. Although these two sets of terms are not synonymous, they are plainly correlative here and have the same frame of reference. This introduction of expressly cosmological language makes explicit the comprehensive dimensions of the contrast.

Verse 47 closely parallels verse 45 by contrasting Adam and Christ, the difference being that now the one is "from earth, earthly," the other "from heaven." These prepositional phrases (ἐκ γῆς, ἐξ οὐρανοῦ) are predicates

---

15. The usual view that Paul is giving a pointed refutation of a Philonic exegesis of Genesis 1 and 2 is rejected by Scroggs, *Last Adam*, pp. 87f.
16. Vos, "Eschatology and the Spirit," p. 231. To read "body" in this verse (so Grosheide, *I Cor.*, p. 387 and Bachmann, *I. Kor.*, p. 469) misses the basic trend of the argument.

and have qualitative force.[17] The latter no more refers to the coming of Christ out of the state of preexistence at his incarnation[18] than the former means that preexistent Adam "came" out of the earth at creation. Besides, such a notion applied to Christ would contradict the principle just laid down in verse 46: not first the pneumatic, but first the psychical then the pneumatic.[19] The parallelism also excludes the notion that "from heaven" refers to the second coming.[20] This qualitative interpretation[21] is confirmed in verses 48 and 49 by the application of the adjective "heavenly" (arising from the use of the prepositional phrase) to believers as well as Christ. It can hardly mean that the former have come out of heaven.[22] Verses 45 and 47 describe states resulting from a becoming that for Adam took place at his creation, for Christ at a point yet to be determined. *Whether or in what condition Christ existed prior to that point is here outside Paul's scope.*

Verses 48 and 49 make plain that Adam and Christ are being compared not simply as individuals. Associated with Adam as *the* earthly one (ὁ χοϊκός) are those of the earthly order; associated with Christ as *the* heavenly one (ὁ ἐπουράνιος) are those of the heavenly order. Moreover, not only their representative capacity but also the *constitutive* nature of their primacy is prominent here. "The earthly ones" are such only as they in solidarity with "the earthly one" bear his image; "the heavenly ones" are such only as they in union with "the heavenly one" bear his image. Verse 49b both brings to a climax the contrast begun in verse 42 and expresses

---

17. So Deissner, *Auferstehungshoffnung und Pneumagedanke bei Paulus*, p. 43; Vos, *Eschatology*, pp. 167f.; Ridderbos, *Paul*, p. 76, n. 110; cf. N. Turner, *Syntax*, J. H. Moulton, *A Grammar of New Testament Greek*, vol. 3 (Edinburgh: T. & T. Clark, 1963), p. 260; M. Zerwick, *Biblical Greek*, Scripta pontificii instituti Biblici, 114 (Rome, 1963), pp. 45f.

18. The view of Hodge (*I Cor.*, p. 352) and Grosheide (*I Cor.*, p. 388).

19. Cf. Vos, *Eschatology*, p. 168.

20. A reference to the second advent is found, e.g., by Bachmann, *I. Kor.*, p. 469 and Robertson-Plummer, *I Cor.*, p. 374; cf. Weiss, *I. Kor.*, p. 376.

21. χοϊκός (v. 47a), which has no parallel in verse 47b, is redundant, emphasizing the qualitative force of the preceding phrase and so of the corresponding phrase in the second half of the verse as well. Weiss (*I Kor.*, p. 376) suggests a reflection here of the language of Genesis 2:7a in the Septuagint: χοῦν ἀπὸ τῆς γῆς.

22. Cf. Vos, *Eschatology*, pp. 167f., n. 18. A similar adjectival use of "from heaven" is found in II Cor. 5:2; cf. Mark 11:30.

the focal consideration in answer to the questions in verse 35: the mode of the resurrection and the nature of the resurrection body are to be explained in terms of union with Christ, the last Adam, as the heavenly one, the life-giving πνεῦμα.[23]

Our findings to this point may be summarized as follows: The contrast between Adam and Christ as living soul and life-giving πνεῦμα, respectively, is not only pointed but also comprehensive and exclusive. They are in view not only as individuals but primarily as heads representing and constituting the existence of others, and hence as representatives of two contrasting orders of life, two aeons, two world-periods, in a word, two creations— the one psychical and earthly, the other, pneumatic and heavenly. Moreover, as the one follows the other, they together span the flow of time. The order of Adam is first (cf. πρῶτος, v. 45); there is none before him. The order of Christ is second (cf. δεύτερος, v. 47); there is none between Adam and Christ. The order of Christ is last (cf. ἐσχατός, v. 45); there is none after Christ. He is the eschatological man; his is the eschatological order.[24]

With this preparatory spadework completed we can now concentrate on the description of Christ as life-giving πνεῦμα in verse 45c. (1) What is the specific reference of πνεῦμα? (2) When did he become life-giving πνεῦμα?

(1) The first question is answered in the light of the correlation between πνεῦμα and the adjective "spiritual" (πνευματικόν, vv. 44b, 46), an especially close correlation in view of the overall structure of the passage and the function of verse 45 in providing proof for verse 44b. In Paul's usage, with the exception of Ephesians 6:12, πνευματικός always has specific reference to the activity of the Holy Spirit (e.g., Rom. 1:11; 7:14; I Cor. 12:1; 14:1; Gal. 6:1; Eph. 1:3; 5:19; Col. 1:9). This is particularly apparent in I Corinthians 2:13-15, the only other place where Paul contrasts πνευματικός with ψυχικός. The main emphasis

---

23. The proximate reference of "the image of the heavenly" is the "spiritual body" of verse 44. Certainly, however, it brings into view more broadly the incorruptible, glorious, powerful character of personal existence in the pneumatic, heavenly order.
24. See Murray, *Imputation*, p. 39; cf. Ridderbos (*Paul*, pp. 60f.) on verse 22: "Adam and Christ here stand over against each other as the two great figures at the entrance of two worlds, two aeons, two 'creations,' the old and the new; and in their actions and fate lies the decision for all who belong to them, because they are comprehended in them and thus are reckoned either to death or to life."

of the immediate context (vv. 10ff.) is the Spirit's function in revelation (cf. v. 4), and repeated reference is made to his person (v. 10 [twice]; vv. 11, 12, 13, 14). The contrast, then, underscores the indispensability of the Spirit's activity. The phrase at the end of verse 13 (πνευματικοῖς πνευματικὰ συγκρίνοντες), whatever its precise meaning, refers to those things and that activity distinguishing the teaching ministry of the Spirit. Accordingly, the "natural man" (ψυχικὸς ἀνθρωπός) is unable to receive "the things of the Spirit of God" because he lacks the corresponding facility of discerning "spiritually" (πνευματικῶς) requisite for understanding them (v. 14). In contrast, "the spiritual man" (ὁ πνευματικός), since he is qualified by the Spirit, possesses such discernment (v. 15; cf. v. 12). All four occurrences in verses 13-15 of "spiritual(ly)" plainly refer to the activity of the Holy Spirit.

Paul's usage elsewhere, then, favors taking "spiritual" in verses 44 and 46 as a reference to the work of the Holy Spirit. This conclusion is supported in the context by its use in verse 44 to describe the resurrection body. As such it sums up the predicates in verses 42f.: incorruption, glory, and power. These according to Paul are always elements in the closely-knit conceptual network whose core is "Spirit."[25] They are only found where the Holy Spirit is at work.

A combination of factors outside verse 45 inevitably points to πνεῦμα as a specific reference to the person of the Holy Spirit. This conclusion is confirmed by the attributive qualifier "life-giving" (ζωοποιοῦν). Without reintroducing what has already been said about the inseparable bond between the Spirit and life, uses of this verb (ζωοποιέω) elsewhere show unquestionably that the Spirit is in view here. God will "give life" to the mortal bodies of believers "through his Spirit" (Rom. 8:11). Even more decisively, II Corinthians 3:6 asserts, with the ring of a general principle: "The Spirit gives life" (cf. John 6:63; I Peter 3:18).[26]

---

25. See above, pp. 69f.
26. The conclusion that the Holy Spirit is in view in verse 45c, although held by Calvin (*The First Epistle of Paul the Apostle to the Corinthians*, trans. J. W. Fraser [Grand Rapids: Eerdmans, 1960], pp. 338f.), is at variance with the standard Reformed commentaries. The position of Grosheide is puzzling. He recognizes that "spiritual" refers to the work of the Spirit. Yet he denies that the noun has reference to his person, maintaining at the same time that Christ does give life through the

Verse 45c, then, teaches that Christ became life-giving Spirit. From the context where Paul's perspective, although broad, remains entirely within the sphere of the historical, this identification is plainly not ontological, as if he were here obliterating the personal distinction between Christ and the Spirit. Such a view would be a too-flagrant contradiction of his uniform teaching elsewhere.[27] Rather, the oneness expressed has in view a conjunction between Christ (as the last *Adam*) and the Spirit dating from a point still to be determined. Christ (as *incarnate*) experiences a spiritual qualification and transformation so thorough, an endowment with the Spirit so complete that as a result they can now be equated. This unprecedented possession of the Spirit and the accompanying change in Christ result in a unity so close that not only can it be said simply that the Spirit makes alive, but also that Christ *as Spirit* makes alive. Specifically, this identity is economic or functional, in terms of their activity, and there is no need to discover "more" than this.[28]

(2) If Christ *became* life-giving Spirit, *when* did that take place? One may be inclined to say that the overall emphasis of the chapter makes it apparent that the answer is Christ's resurrection. However, representative Reformed exegesis favors the incarnation,[29] and so an effort must be made to settle the issue.

Spirit (*I Cor.*, p. 387). The view of Hodge is more consistent but even less true to Paul. He understands both noun and adjective as referring to the "principle of rational life" (*I Cor.*, p. 348), "rational and immortal soul" (p. 350), in contrast to "soul" understood as the "principle of animal life" (p. 348). Whether the latter, either in its usage in this passage or in Genesis 2:7, can be restricted in such a fashion is highly doubtful. Hodge's discussion as a whole shows that the analogy of Paul's usage and the structure of his teaching have been obscured by the controlling influence of what "has ever been a fundamental principle of Christian anthropology," namely, that "the Bible recognizes in man only two subjects or distinct separable substances, the soul and body" (p. 348).

27. See above, pp. 71-73.

28. Versteeg (*Christus en de Geest*, esp. pp. 381-389, cf. pp. 91, 412) prefers the term "eschatological" to describe this unity. The comment of N. Q. Hamilton (*The Holy Spirit and Eschatology in Paul*, p. 15) is unwarranted and certainly not supported by his own exegesis: "Here we see the Spirit and Christ identified in a remarkably intimate way which goes beyond all dynamic explanations."

29. So Hodge, *I Cor.*, pp. 350ff.; Grosheide, *I Cor.*, p. 387; cf. the indefinite comment of L. Morris, *The First Epistle of Paul to the Corinthians*, The Tyndale New Testament Commentaries, ed. R. V. G. Tasker (Grand Rapids: Eerdmans, 1958), p. 229: "Some see a reference to the incarnation, others to the resurrection or the second advent. But Paul is not specific."

This can be done most easily by referring to verses 20-
22. The close affinity of verse 22 with verse 45 is obvious:
both contain not only the same explicit contrast between
Adam and Christ but also on the christological side the
same verbal idea—"making alive." Earlier we noted the
sequence of amplification in these verses:[30] Verse 21 ex-
pands on verse 20 and verse 22, in turn, on verse 21. Consequently, the "making alive" of all in Christ (the
resurrection of the dead through him, v. 21) is here
grounded specifically in his resurrection and, by inference, what he is by virtue of that resurrection (v. 20).[31]
An integral connection exists between Christ as firstfruits
and Christ as life-giving Spirit. In fact, because Christ's
resurrection is the indispensable foundation for others to
share in resurrection life, he functions as life-giving Spirit
only on the basis of his resurrection, only in his resurrected state. Specifically the resurrected Christ is the
life-giving Christ. The plain implication, then, is that the
last Adam became life-giving Spirit at his resurrection.

This conclusion is reinforced by the functioning of the
"firstfruits" principle in the immediate context of verse
45. As already noted, verse 45 at the very least introduces
Christ, the last Adam, as the model spiritual man. His
fuller significance as life-giving inevitably involves that
he is the primary exemplification of the spiritual existence which he communicates to the rest of the harvest.
Now since the (bodily) spiritual existence of believers
begins at their resurrection (v. 44), in view of the
solidarity involved, Christ's spiritual existence, his
becoming life-giving Spirit, dates from the resurrection.

To argue this point at length only serves to obscure it. It
is neither by virtue of his preexistence or because of his
incarnation that the last Adam is life-giving Spirit. The
final word in this connection has been spoken by Deissner:

> As a matter of fact, it would have made no sense to construct the
> argumentation in chapter 15 on the resurrection of Christ, if

---

30. See above, p. 36.
31. The perfect tense of the verb in verse 20 confirms this inference.

Christ were already qualified as the giver of life by virtue of his origin or by virtue of his capacity as preexistent heavenly man.[32]

Conclusions. (1) At his resurrection the personal mode of Jesus' existence as the last Adam was so decisively transformed by the Holy Spirit that Paul says he has become life-giving Spirit. The Spirit, who raised him up as the firstfruits, indwells him so completely and in such a fashion that in their functioning he *is* the Spirit who will be instrumental in the resurrection of the full harvest. Further, (a) the life-giving activity predicated of the resurrected Christ, is not predicated *directly*; the Spirit is an absolutely indispensable factor. Only by virtue of the functional identity of the Spirit and Christ, effected redemptive-historically in his resurrection, is Christ the communicator of life. No principle in Paul's soteriology is more fundamental. (b) The change in Christ's person at his resurrection is as real as and commensurate with the transformation to be experienced by the rest of the harvest.[33]

(2) The resurrection of Jesus has more than personal significance. Verse 45 in its immediate context brings into view not only an organic connection with the resurrection of believers but also considerations cosmic in scope. Resurrection is here nothing less than the counterpart of creation. The resurrection of Christ is the beginning of the new and final world-order, an order described as spiritual and heavenly. It is the dawn of the new creation,

---

32. *Auferstehungshoffnung*, p. 40; cf. Herman, *Kyrios und Pneuma*, pp. 61f.; Guntermann, *Eschatologie*, p. 174; F. Büchsel, *Der Geist Gottes im Neuen Testament* (Gütersloh: C. Bertelsmann, 1926), p. 406; J. Jervell, *Imago Dei. Gen. 1,26f. im Spätjudentum, in der Gnosis und in den paulinischen Briefen* (Göttingen: Vandenhoeck & Ruprecht, 1960), p. 268.

33. Cf. the following comments of Vos on Rom. 1:4 also applied by him to I Cor. 15:45-49: "According to Rom. 1:1-4, while the identical Jesus who had been buried rose from the grave, yet it was by no means the same Jesus in the endowment and equipment of his human nature. Not only a new status had been acquired through the resurrection: new qualities amounting to a reconstructed adjustment to the future heavenly environment had been wrought in Him by the omnipotent power of God: He had been determined (declared effectually) the Son of God with power according to the Spirit of Holiness, by the resurrection from the dead. It is self-evident that these words do not refer to any religious or ethical transformation which Jesus in the resurrection had to undergo. Such a thought nowhere finds support in Paul's Christology, nor in his general teaching. Only, in the quite justifiable eagerness for excluding this, there is too narrow an interpretation put upon the sentence, as though it meant to affirm a purely bodily transformation. The other, psychical, side of our Lord's human nature was obviously affected no less than the physical side. This comprehensive change was inseparable from the resurrection itself; it was not an additional element, but an integral part of the first and only act required" (*Eschatology*, pp. 209f.).

the start of the eschatological age. In terms of the conceptual the start of the Paul views the whole of history, it is the commencement of the "age-to-come."[34]

Such a broad perspective has far-reaching implications:

(a) In this passage "spiritual," "last," and "heavenly" are clearly correlative. Verse 46 in particular expresses the essential tie between the Spirit and the eschatological, heavenly world (cf. Eph. 1:3). The final order is a specifically pneumatic order. Its atmosphere, as it were, is spiritual. So far as individual eschatological existence is concerned, the Spirit is not only active in its inception but completely dominates the resultant state. In fact, Paul's thought appears to move from the Spirit's constitutive place in the resurrected life to his role in the act of resurrection, rather than the reverse.[35] Because he so thoroughly conditions the former, he is appropriately instrumental in the latter.

(b) Perhaps the most distinctive mark of Paul's conception of the Spirit and his activity is its eschatological aspect, dominant in this passage. Yet it is often overlooked.[36] Few misunderstandings of Paul are more widespread than the tendency to consider his teaching on the Spirit, particularly the Spirit's present sanctifying work in the believer, without reference to his eschatology. This tendency seems in large part chargeable to the *loci* method of dogmatics in confining the locus of eschatology to dealing with the "last things," understood as all that dates from the second coming of Christ (the lone exception being the intermediate state, treated in individual eschatology). According to this passage, how-

---

34. "The whole tenor of the argument (for such it actually is) compels us to think of the resurrection as the moment at which τὸ πνευματικόν entered. Christ appeared then and there in the form of a πνευματικός and as such inaugurated the eschatological era" (Vos, *Eschatology*, p. 168; cf. "Eschatology and the Spirit," p. 233); "As Adam stands at the head of the αἰὼν οὗτος as the first man, so the risen Christ stands at the head of the αἰὼν μέλλων as the Initiator of the perfect redeemed creation of God" (J. Jeremias, *TDNT*, 1:143); cf. Jervell, *Imago Dei*, p. 268.
35. Cf. Vos, *Eschatology*, pp. 169ff.
36. Vos ("Eschatology and the Spirit") is the first to show the importance of this aspect for the whole of Paul's theology (cf. *Eschatology*, esp. pp. 58-60, 159-171). This has subsequently been generally recognized; cf., e.g., Hamilton, *Holy Spirit and Eschatology*; Koch, "L'aspect eschatologique"; R. C. Oudersluys, "Eschatology and the Holy Spirit," *The Reformed Review*, 19(1965):3-12.

ever, "eschatology" dates from Christ's resurrection. The issue here it not merely semantic.[37] Traditional dogmatics by its very structure obscures the structure and important perspectives of Paul's theology. It masks the outlook basic not only to Paul but the entire New Testament that the Messiah's coming is one (eschatological) coming which unfolds in two episodes, one already and one still to come, that the "age-to-come" is not only future but present.[38] It veils the organic connection between the resurrection of Christ (in which, according to this passage, the redemptive-historical significance of the first coming is concentrated) and the bodily resurrection of believers (=second coming). Further, the conventional dogmatic outlook eclipses the eschatological quality of the believer's present soteriological experience, the integral bond between present and future in the life of those joined to the resurrected Christ.[39]

(3) This passage sheds light on the way Paul relates Christ's resurrection to his ascension (and heavenly session). Clearly he views them as separate occurrences. In Romans 8:34 being at the right hand of God is distinguished from being raised.[40] The act of ascension as distinct from the act of resurrection is the plain presupposition. The same observation applies in Ephesians 1:20 and 2:6 where being raised and being seated in the heavenlies are distinguished. Accordingly, the same distinction is implicit in Philippians 2:9 where exaltation

---

37. For a helpful discussion of the different uses of "eschatology" and "eschatological" in contemporary discussion and the equivocation possible, cf. K. Kertelge, *"Rechfertigung" bei Paulus*, NA, Neue Folge, 3 (Münster: Aschendorff, 1967), pp. 129-131.

38. This perspective is reflected, e.g., in the structure of Jesus' kingdom proclamation.

39. A brief but excellent treatment of the interpenetration of eschatology and soteriology in Paul is given by Vos, *Eschatology*, Chapter II (pp. 42-61). It ought to be recognized in this connection that the judgment of P. Stuhlmacher (*Gerechtigkeit Gottes bei Paulus* [Göttingen: Vandenhoeck & Ruprecht, 1965], p. 12) may be validly extended to include most of subsequent church history: "The eschatology of the Apostolic Fathers no longer recognizes the Pauline overlap of both aeons in the present, therefore also no longer recognizes the eschatological tension of present and future, but expects only a (more or less) prolonged future."

40. This is especially clear if καί is read before ἐστιν in the first relative clause as the more difficult reading (cf. E. Schäder, *Die Bedeutung des lebendigen Christus für die Rechtfertigung nach Paulus*, p. 183, n. 1). It is omitted by Nestle-Aland (25th ed.), Kilpatrick (2nd ed.) and Souter (2nd ed.), but included in UBS (3rd ed.).

(without mention of resurrection) is set over against obedience unto death (v. 8).

The resurrection, however, has a more than temporal priority. Verse 45 together with verses 47-49 makes it unavoidably clear that Christ's resurrection is integral to his subsequent mode of existence. What Christ is and continues to be he became at the resurrection and at no other point. The exalted, pneumatic, heavenly existence of the second Adam is specifically his existence as life-giving Spirit. Ascension and heavenly session are exponential of resurrection. Certainly Paul gives no indication that the former effected changes in Christ's exalted person not experienced at the latter.

II Corinthians 3:17

"The Lord is the $\pi\nu\epsilon\hat{\upsilon}\mu\alpha$." Differences in the understanding of this statement are perennial.[41] Our concern here is to examine it briefly against the background of I Corinthians 15:45 in order to determine how the two statements are related. This can be done by answering two questions: What is the nature of this identification, and on what is it based?

(1) No small degree of the difficulty with this verse comes from the failure to appreciate adequately its integral place in the context. It is not an "incidental remark."[42] Such an assessment improperly isolates this statement with its admittedly general tone, investing it with an indefiniteness which, in turn, gives rise to all kinds of uncontrolled speculation. What is the function of verse 17 in the context?

In the section 3:1—4:6, Paul is intent on the defense of his personal integrity and apostleship.[43] This is apparent in the opening verses of chapter 3. Paul does not commend himself nor does he need letters of commendation

---

41. For a slightly dated but good summary of the different interpretations, see P. Bachmann, *Der zweite Brief des Paulus an die Korinther*, ZahnK, 8, 4th ed. (Leipzig: A. Deichert, 1922), pp. 172f., n. 1; cf. D. R. Griffiths, " 'The Lord is the Spirit,' " *Expository Times*, 55 (1943-44): 81f.; Hermann (*Kyrios und Pneuma*, pp. 17-19) carries the survey into the past decade.

42. "Zwischenbemerkung," H. Windisch, *Der zweite Korintherbrief*, p. 124. Alfred Plummer writes with reference to the two clauses of v. 17, "They might be omitted without loss to the arguments . . ." *A Critical and Exegetical Commentary of the Second Epistle of St. Paul to the Corinthians*, ICC (New York: Scribner's Sons, 1915), p. 102.

43. The origin and character of the opposition in view need not concern us here.

(v. 1), because the Corinthian believers themselves are such a letter (v. 2). In particular, the notion that they are "a letter of Christ ministered to by us" (v. 3) is a key to understanding not only the immediate but broader context. For its amplification influences the discussion to the end of the section. This can be seen provisionally in the recurrence of the vocabulary for ministry (here the verb διακονέω) throughout. In verse 6 Paul identifies himself as a "minister" (διάκονος) of the new covenant, and the verses immediately following (7-11) unfold around the fundamental contrast between the two "ministries" (διακονία). The occurrence of the same noun in 4:1 is an indication that Paul is still thinking in terms of this contrast at that point.

The letter mentioned in verse 3 is further described as written not with ink but "with the Spirit of the living God." Apparently no one disputes that this refers to the Holy Spirit. This being the case two important observations follow: (1) At this juncture, pivotal for the passage as a whole, Christ and the Holy Spirit are closely conjoined in terms of redemptive activity. (2) In view here is a contrast in which on the one side the Spirit has a distinguishing role.

This second observation is important for determining the references in verse 6. For, while the contrast here has a broader, explicitly covenantal scope, it can hardly be other than an expansion of the contrast already introduced in verse 3. Therefore, the two occurrences of πνεῦμα refer specifically to the Holy Spirit.[44] In view here of the inseparable tie between the Spirit and life, this conclusion is confirmed by the generalization at the end of the verse: "the πνεῦμα gives life" (cf. Rom. 8:2, 6, 10; 7:6 with 6:4; I Cor. 15:45).

---

44. The view of Charles Hodge that the usage here and in verse 8 "evidently means the gospel" rests on the failure to grasp sufficiently its connection with the use in verse 3 (*An Exposition of the Second Epistle to the Corinthians* [New York: Robert Carter and Brothers, 1866]), p. 61; cf. pp. 55, 56). The position of Philip Hughes (*Second Corinthians*, p. 101) is similar. Explicitly rejecting that a direct reference to the Holy Spirit is intended, he appeals to verse 3 (where he himself recognizes that Paul is speaking of the Spirit) to support the idea that rather "what is internal" is in view. Although in the context, on the one side of the contrast, the gospel or an internal writing of the law is certainly in view, this consideration may not obscure the pointedness of Paul's own usage and his redemptive-historical orientation.

The wider perspective expressed in this verse makes clearer the nature of this contrast in which the Spirit figures so prominently. It is certainly not based on the "'Marcionite' antithesis" between a written and an unwritten code.[45] Nor is it fundamentally an antithesis between the law as externally and internally written, that is, between law and gospel.[46] Rather it is pointedly *historical* in character. For it is a contrast between covenants, a contrast between successive phases in the history of redemption, between the old order and the new in which the latter is distinguished by the work of the Spirit.[47] Verse 6 strengthens the first observation made above on verse 3, namely, that in the context Paul's interest in the Spirit (and Christ) is historical, that is, in terms of contrasting covenantal administration ($\delta\iota\alpha\vartheta\dot{\eta}\kappa\eta$).

Verses 7-11, with their antithetically parallel structure, clearly develop the contrast outlined in verse 6. So far as personal exponents are concerned, the Spirit is associated with the new covenant in contrast with Moses and the old. The former covenant as the ministry of the Spirit is a ministry of life[48] and righteousness; the latter, a ministry of death and condemnation (vv. 7-9). The glory of the new outshines that of the old as if the latter had none (vv. 10f.). Again, note that this (historical) concern with ministries (and covenants) is still in Paul's mind in 4:1.

Although they do not display the same antithetical parallelism, verses 12ff. continue the contrast. On the one hand, they explain why the old covenant, the ministry of Moses, the reading of the law, was a ministry of condemnation and death—because of the hardened minds of the sons of Israel (v. 14), because a veil lies over their hearts (v. 15). On the other hand, the ground for the efficacy of the new covenant is indicated: the veil is removed in

---

45. So Windisch, *II. Kor.*, pp. 110f.; cf. Plummer, *II Cor.*, pp. 87-89.
46. So, e.g., Hodge and Hughes, see above, n. 44.
47. That in the final analysis Paul's interest in these verses is redemptive-historical and not in terms of *ordo salutis* is confirmed by the sharpness of the antithesis. He is hardly contradicting his teaching elsewhere and saying that the individual Old Testament believer did not experience the inward, transforming work of the Spirit; cf. esp. I Cor. 10:3f.
48. This can be inferred from the parallelism in which $\pi\nu\epsilon\dot{\upsilon}\mu\alpha\tau\sigma\varsigma$ (v. 8) is the counterpart of $\vartheta\alpha\nu\dot{\alpha}\tau\sigma\upsilon$ (v. 7), which also confirms that the Holy Spirit is in view.

Christ (v. 14), taken away, when Israel[49] turns to the Lord (v. 16).

Summarizing the central features of our survey, the redemptive-historical contrast intimated in verse 3 and defined broadly in terms of the old and new covenants (v. 6) is developed in verses 7ff., where the superiority and surpassing glory of the new order are expressed personally by the contrast between the Spirit and Moses. At verse 12, however, a shift takes place. Now the superiority and efficacy of the new are indicated by the personal contrast between Christ and Moses. This shift, then, prompts the question: if the surpassing glory, life, and righteousness of the new covenant result from its being a ministry of the *Spirit*, how can they be attributed in effect to *Christ*, to the Lord? What warrants this shift?[50]

The integral function of verse 17a in the context is to provide the answer to this question; i.e., because the Lord is the Spirit.[51] Paul makes the preceding shift from the Spirit to Christ, because *in terms of the efficacy of the new covenant*, they are one. The conjunction between Christ and the Spirit already indicated in verse 3 (and so, continually in the background) is here made most explicit and intimate: in terms of their redemptive activity, they are identified.[52]

49. Most probably the unexpressed subject of the verb "turns"; cf. Hughes, *II Cor.*, p. 113, n. 10 for a summary of the various interpretations.

50. The occurrences of "Lord" in verse 17 (and 18) derive from the Old Testament language utilized in verse 16. The latter, however, is qualified by "in Christ" (v. 14). Hence all five instances refer to Christ. This is confirmed by the fact that the glory of the Lord which transforms believers, as they behold it, into the *same image* (v. 18) is none other than the glory of Christ, who is *the image* of God (4:4), the glory of God which is only to be had in the face of Christ (4:6; cf. Rom. 8:29; I Cor. 15:49).

51. In other words, δέ (17a) has explanatory force; cf. Hodge, *II Cor.*, p. 73. From the context τὸ πνεῦμα is clearly the predicate, not the subject; cf. F. W. Grosheide, *De Tweede Brief aan de Kerk te Korinthe*, CNT, 2nd ed. (Kampen: J. H. Kok, 1959), pp. 108f.

52. Hughes, in keeping with his understanding of verse 6, finds here a reference to (Christ as) "the source of light and life" (*II Cor.*, p. 115). However, the remark made a little later concerning this verse is highly revealing: "Although, however, there is in our judgment no *direct* reference to the Holy Spirit here, yet there can be no doubt that the operation of the Holy Spirit is implicit in Paul's argument. . . . The distinction between 'spirit' and 'Spirit' accordingly becomes a fine one . . ." (p. 116f.). Is the distinction there at all? Hodge, less consistently (see above, n. 44), sees that the references in verse 17 are to the Holy Spirit (*II Cor.*, pp. 74f.).

In view of the integral place of verse 17a in this passage with its pervasive historical orientation, it is clearly unwarranted to understand this equation ontologically.[53] By the same token the elements of thought found in I Corinthians 15:45 are present here: an integration in the exercise of redemptive functions expressed as oneness, and a oneness, in turn, resting on a pneumatic transformation of Christ's person so thorough that he and the Spirit are identified. The Lord is the Spirit because he *became* life-giving Spirit.

Verses 17b and 18 substantiate this economic interpretation. "The Spirit of the Lord" (17b) expresses a distinction showing that the equation just made is not intended in an absolute, ontological sense. And the mention of freedom clearly maintains the functional tone. Along with glory, righteousness, and life, it is one of the blessings of the new covenant closely associated with the work of the Spirit (Rom. 8:2; cf. Gal. 4:21-5:1; 5:13 with 5:16ff.). Similarly, the transformation of believers described in verse 18 (cf. the removal of the veil, vv. 14, 16) takes place ἀπὸ κυρίου πνεύματος. However exactly the two nouns in this phrase are to be related,[54] they bring into view a close conjunction between Christ and the Spirit in the work of redemption, a conjunction explained by the equation of verse 17a.

(2) On what is this functional identification in verse 17 based? If this oneness has a redemptive-historical character, when does it begin? This question can only be answered in the light of the affinity with I Corinthians 15:45 already noted. Both verses are pivotal in contrasts where a redemptive-historical outlook is determinative, functioning to explain the dynamic in the realization of the final order, the new creation. Seen in their respective contexts, I Corinthians 15:45c and II Corinthians 3:17a are closely correlative so that it is difficult to evade the conclusion that the identification expressed in the latter dates from Jesus' resurrection. Because at his resurrection he became life-giving Spirit, now he is the Spirit.

53. So, e.g., Hodge, as representative of a long tradition before him: "It is an identity of essence and power." (*II Cor.*, p. 74). Cf. Hamilton, *Holy Spirit and Eschatology*, p. 6: "The identity here posited is not ontological, an identity of being, but dynamic, an identity which occurs in redemptive action."
54. Cf. Hughes, *II Cor.*, p. 120, n. 23 for a list of the different suggestions.

This conclusion is confirmed in the immediate context. The new covenant glory emphasized throughout (vv. 7-11, esp. 10, 11, 18; 4:4, 6)[55] and its concommitants—life, righteousness, and liberty, derive from the Lord, who is the Spirit (vv. 17f.; 4:4-6). Now I Corinthians 15:42ff. show clearly that the bestowal of these benefits depends on the last Adam as he has been invested with glory and made life-giving Spirit at the resurrection. Accordingly, while the resurrection is not mentioned explicitly, 3:1—4:6 is an extended witness to the dependence of the blessings given under the new covenant on the glorified and living Christ, that is, the Christ who is what he is by virtue of resurrection.

Conclusion. The centrality of the historical factor in I Corinthians 15:45 and II Corinthians 3:17 needs to be emphasized especially in view of the abiding tendency to read Paul in terms of dogmatic conceptions which, although in themselves biblical, obscure this point. The identity affirmed in these verses is not an aspect of the eternal, ontological relationship between Christ and the Spirit. It is not "an identity of essence and power" (Hodge).[56] Rather it is a being one which is based on a *becoming* one, a oneness of the Spirit and the last Adam (the *incarnate* Son) dating from his resurrection. It is a functional, dynamic identity. Consequently, the unity of Christ and the Spirit in saving activity is not to be delineated exclusively in terms of their common divinity and eternity. Where this is not appreciated, the historical character of redemption so basic for Paul is seriously undercut. An ontological interest has a definite place in Paul's christology, as we shall presently see, but to read these verses primarily in terms of that interest results in an impoverished understanding of his soteriology as a whole.

55. Note that my remarks here and elsewhere have reference specifically to the eschatological, soteriological, pneumatic glory which dates from Jesus' resurrection. Paul does employ the notion in a broader, less pointed sense (e.g., Rom. 1:23; I Cor. 11:7, 15; 15:40). However, the pattern of usage justifies the kind of discrimination made above. Cf. Vos, *Eschatology*, pp. 302ff.

56. Cf. Grosheide's treatment of II Cor. 3:17 which has a certain vagueness because of his failure to grasp this point sufficiently and make the necessary distinctions (*II Cor.*, pp. 108-110).

Romans 1:3, 4

These verses provide a number of interesting and difficult problems. Linguistic and stylistic peculiarities, a compressed mode of expression, and syntactical difficulties all combine in a statement relatively independent in its context. Our interest here is to explore what they say about the christological and soteriological significance of the resurrection. Preliminary to this, however, two matters need to be dealt with briefly.

(1) Form criticism of the New Testament, applied initially to Revelation and the synoptic gospels, has in recent years been extended increasingly to the other books. In particular, it has found in Paul's letters liturgical material of pre-Pauline origin (primarily confessional formulas and hymns),[57] and there is extensive agreement that Romans 1:3, 4 are among this material or, at least, that a pre-Pauline confessional formula visibly underlies them.[58]

Without attempting here to assess these developments in any detail, two reservations need to be discussed. These apply as well to other passages to be treated below, such as Romans 4:25; Philippians 2:6-11 and I Timothy 3:16.

(a) While Paul may well have taken over materials already in use in the church, the highly tentative character of specific conclusions to that effect ought to be apparent. One is limited almost exclusively to inferences drawn from the text itself. Further, in any given instance those finding a pre-Pauline formulation disagree on what, if any, modifications Paul has made.[59] Moreover, while acceptance of the general theory is widespread, its application has also been broadly challenged.[60]

---

57. E.g., J. Reumann ("The Gospel of the Righteousness of God," *Interpretation*, 20 [1966]:432-452) approves the view that Romans is "a sort of commentary on such formulas" and claims that "all of the first eight chapters are thus structured around Pauline exposition of creedal formulas" (p. 432). Cf. for general discussion of the topic, E. Käsemann, "Liturgische Formeln im NT," *Die Religion in Geschichte und Gegenwart*, 3rd ed. (Tübingen: J. C. B. Mohr, 1958), 2:993-996.

58. E.g., Bultmann, *Theology*, 1:50; E. Schweizer, *Erniedrigung und Erhöhung bei Jesu und seinen Nachfolgern*, pp. 55f., 62f., 101; Michel, *an die Römer*, pp. 30f.; Kramer *Christ, Lord, Son of God*, pp. 108-111. Kramer provides a short summary of the grounds for this position.

59. Cf. the differences among the works cited in the two preceding footnotes.

60. Cf. G. Delling, "Zum neueren Paulusverständnis," *Novum Testamentum*, 4 (1960):98; V. S. Poythress, "Is Romans 1:3-4 a *Pauline* Confession After All?" *The Expository Times*, 87(1975-76):180-183.

(b) A form-critical approach must not become a vehicle for intruding nonexistent discontinuities into the text, either within Paul's epistles or between him and those from whom he presumably borrowed.[61] Even if the origin of a text be pre-Pauline, this in itself does not make it less properly Paul's or less integral to his teaching. If anything, it shows, as he himself insisted (Gal. 2:1-10), that he agrees with those who preceded him in the faith and witnesses to the unity of early Christian belief. Romans 1:3f., then, may be approached as providing teaching that is fully Paul's.

(2) While these verses are a relatively self-contained unit tempting one to an isolated treatment of them, insight into their place in the immediate context, particularly what precedes, is important for understanding them overall. These verses have their place in the opening section (vv. 1-7) which conforms in basic format to the letter-writing practice of the day. However, in keeping with his custom elsewhere (notably Galatians and Titus), Paul does not follow this form slavishly but improvises and interpolates, thereby highlighting considerations relevant to developments in the body of the letter.

Specifically, the nominative section of the *exordium* here is extensively expanded (vv. 1b-6). As the last of three appositional qualifications, Paul identifies himself as "set apart for the gospel of God" (v. 1). This, in turn, gives rise to the relative clause (v. 2) expressing the continuity of this gospel with the Old Testament revelation, and the reference to God's Son (v. 3) as the content of the gospel.[62] Mention of the Son, in turn, is the occasion for the two participial clauses (vv. 3, 4) and the relative clause in verse 5. Verse 6, in turn, flows out of verse 5. Syntactically, then, verses 3f. are woven tightly into the fabric of the im-

---

61. Cf. the following comments of C. H. Dodd on Rom. 1:3f.: "This is scarcely a statement of Paul's own theology. . . . The present statement therefore falls short of what Paul would regard as an adequate doctrine of the Person of Christ. . . . It is probable that Paul is citing more or less exactly a common confession of faith which would be known and recognized at Rome" (*The Epistle of Paul to the Romans*, The Moffat New Testament Commentary (London: Hodder and Stoughton, 1932), pp. 4f.).

62. Even if the prepositional phrase περὶ τοῦ υἱοῦ αὐτοῦ is to be taken adverbially with the verb in verse 2 rather than attributively with εὐαγγέλιον (v. 1), it still specifies the subject matter of the gospel; cf. Murray, *Romans*, 1:5.

mediate context. They consist of two clauses, each governed by a participle, with both participles functioning attributively as they modify "Son" (v. 3a), which, in turn, specifies the content of "gospel" (v. 1).

In closing off preliminary discussion of these verses, it will be useful to note the obvious parallelism between the two clauses. The pattern of correspondence is as follows:[63]

verse 3	verse 4
"born" (γενομένου)	"declared" (ὁρισθέντος)
"according to the flesh"	"according to the Spirit of holiness"
(κατὰ σάρκα)	(κατὰ πνεῦμα ἁγιωσύνης)
"of the seed of David"	"by the resurrection of the dead"
(ἐκ σπέρματος Δαυίδ)	(ἐξ ἀναστάσεως νεκρῶν)

The expression "Son of God in power" (υἱοῦ θεοῦ ἐν δυνάμει) depends on the participle immediately preceding and creates an imbalance more apparent than real.

In the Reformed tradition these verses have been given either one of two basic, significantly differing interpretations, and we may properly speak of them as the older and newer Reformed interpretations. The former holds that the primary interest of these verses is ontological or metaphysical so that the contrast is between two component parts or coexisting sides in the constitution of Christ's person. This is the view of Calvin,[64] maintained representatively by Charles Hodge,[65] and defended in a vigorous and programmatic fashion by B. B. Warfield.[66] The newer interpretation, while not denying an underlying ontological element, maintains that a redemptive-historical outlook is dominant and that the contrast is between two successive stages or modes of existence. This is the view introduced by Vos[67] and set forth in the

63. Cf. Vos, "Eschatology and the Spirit," p. 228.
64. *The Epistles of Paul the Apostle to the Romans and to the Thessalonians*, trans. R. Mackenzie (Grand Rapids: Eerdmans, 1961), pp. 15-17.
65. *Romans*, pp. 24-30.
66. "The Christ that Paul Preached." It is puzzling that this work, perhaps the most extended exegetical treatment of these verses, appears to have escaped the attention of the commentators.
67. "Eschatology and the Spirit," pp. 228-230; cf. *Eschatology*, pp. 155f., n. 10. The primary stimulus to Vos's thinking at this point appears to have come from Sokolowski (*Geist und Leben*, pp. 56-62), although among Reformed interpreters the rudiments of this view are already present in G. Smeaton, *The Doctrine of the Holy Spirit*, 2nd ed. (Edinburgh: T. & T. Clark, 1889), p. 77.

commentaries of Greijdanus,[68] Ridderbos,[69] and Murray.[70]

Orienting our own exposition to this difference of opinion we will (1) state more fully the older point of view, (2) note its principal shortcomings, and (3) discuss in what ways the newer interpretation provides a more satisfactory alternative.

(1) In the position of Hodge and Warfield two considerations are pivotal. One derives from the broader biblical context, the other from the parallel structure of the two clauses. (a) Hodge and Warfield maintain that biblical usage elsewhere, without exception, demands that "Son of God" (v. 4) refers specifically to Christ's deity.[71] (b) They stress that "flesh" (v. 3) must refer to his humanity so that by virtue of the parallelism between the clauses, "Spirit of holiness" describes his divinity.[72] These two factors, then, converge on the conclusion that the contrast is between the two fundamental components in the make-up of Christ's person—his divine and human natures, and that these verses show Paul to be an explicit advocate of the doctrine of the two natures.[73]

---

68. S. Greijdanus, *De Brief van de Apostel Paulus aan de Gemeente te Rome*, KNT, 6 (Amsterdam: H. A. Van Bottenburg, 1933), 1:58-66.

69. *Romeinen*, pp. 24-26.

70. *Romans*, 1:5-12.

71. Hodge, *Romans*, p. 25: "The term expresses the relation of the second to the first person in the Trinity, as it exists from eternity. It is therefore, as applied to Christ, not a term of office, nor expressive of any relation assumed in time. He was and is the Eternal Son." Warfield, "Paul's Christ," p. 239: "The designation 'Son of God' is a metaphysical designation and tells us what He is in His being of being. And what it tells us that Christ is in His being of being is that He is just what God is" (cf. p. 247). A significant indication of the outlook Hodge brings to bear on this passage is the statement which closes his discussion of this point: "The historical sense of the terms λόγος, εἰκών, υἱός, πρωτότοκος, as learned from the Scriptures and the *usus loquendi* of the apostolic age, shows that they must, in their application to Christ, be understood of his Divine nature." Such a conclusion cannot be squared with the differentiated character of the New Testament usage. See esp. Rom. 8:29; II Cor. 3:18; 4:6; I Cor. 15:49 and Col. 1:18.

72. "That the word σάρξ here means *human nature* is obvious both from the scriptural usage of the word, and from the nature of the case." "As σάρξ means his human nature, πνεῦμα can hardly mean anything else than his higher or divine nature . . . the θεότης, divine nature, or Godhead" (Hodge, pp. 26, 28). "When Paul tells us of the Christ which he preached that He was made of the seed of David 'according to the flesh,' he quite certainly has the whole of His humanity in mind." "Since the 'according to the flesh' includes all His humanity, the 'according to the Spirit of holiness' which is set in contrast with it, . . . must be sought outside of His humanity." ". . . the Spirit of holiness is a designation of His divine nature" (Warfield, p. 247; cf. p. 249).

73. "Paul's whole assertion therefore amounts to saying that, in one element of His being, the Christ that he preached was man, in another God." "But he declares

Several features are characteristic particularly of Warfield's presentation of this position. While recognizing
that "there is a temporal succession suggested in the
declarations of the two clauses" (p. 240), he maintains that
this "emerges merely as the incidental, or we may say
even the accidental result of their collocation"; he adds
that "the relation in which Paul sets the two declarations
to one another is a *logical* rather than a temporal one" (p.
241, my italics). A little later this point is stressed again:
"Temporal succession was not what it was in Paul's mind
to emphasize, and is not the ruling idea of his assertion"
(p. 244).

In connection with this last statement Warfield dis-
cusses the place of the resurrection in these verses. Paul
has so little interest in the temporal factor that "It is quite
indifferent to his declaration when the resurrection took
place" (p. 244). Not too surprisingly, then, the significance of the resurrection resides exclusively in its
noetic function with reference to the divine nature of
Christ. It is important "because of the demonstration it
brought of the dignity of His person," because "it brought
out into plain view who and what Christ really was" (p.
244).[74] Further, he emphatically rejects the idea that the
resurrection is "the producing cause of a change in our
Lord's mode of being" (p. 244); in fact, Warfield states
that "nothing could be more monstrous" than this view
(p. 245). And more than once he repudiates the broader
notion that Paul is contrasting successive stages of existence. "Paul is not here distinguishing times and contrasting two successive modes of our Lord's being. He is
distinguishing elements in the constitution of our Lord's
person" (p. 246).[75] The negative factor supporting Warfield's argument at this point is his view that "flesh" and

Christ to be the promised Messiah and the very Son of God in language so preg-
nant, so packed with implications, as to carry us into the heart of the great problem
of the two-natured person of Christ" (Warfield, pp. 248, 240; cf. p. 250).

74. Cf. pp. 243, 252. See also the comments of Hodge on "declared" (v. 4) as it
describes the resurrection. It is to be understood "declaratively, or in reference to
the knowledge of men," "in view of men, thus determined" (*Romans*, p. 27).

75. Cf. pp. 243, 245, 249f. Is it possible to see in these statements in particular and
in the article as a whole a sharp rejection of the position expressed six years earlier
by his Princeton colleague Vos ("Eschatology and the Spirit," pp. 228ff.)? Warfield
uses no footnotes and does not indicate the direction of his polemic except for
several rather oblique references to the views of Wilhelm Bousset (pp. 235, 237,
239, 250).

"Spirit" are not temporal qualifications and that the phrases containing them here are "ill-adapted to express this temporal distinction" (pp. 244f.).

(2) At first glance the interpretation of Hodge and Warfield may seem quite satisfactory and to have a great deal to commend it. More careful examination, however, uncovers three major objections, each in itself formidable and which together make it unacceptable.

(a) Perhaps the greatest difficulty is that this position takes $\pi\nu\epsilon\hat{\upsilon}\mu\alpha$ (v. 4) to refer to Christ's divine nature.[76] This is entirely without support elsewhere in Paul's writings and preaching. Moreover, $\pi\nu\epsilon\hat{\upsilon}\mu\alpha$ is here set in contrast with $\sigma\acute{\alpha}\rho\xi$, a contrast which elsewhere in Paul refers almost invariably on the one side to the Holy Spirit (e.g., Rom. 8:4-9, 13; Gal. 5:16-26; 6:8; Phil. 3:3f.), the only exceptions being two uses of $\pi\nu\epsilon\hat{\upsilon}\mu\alpha$ in an anthropological sense (I Cor. 5:5; II Cor. 7:1), which obviously does not apply here.[77]

Both Hodge and Warfield try to remove this objection by pointing to the genitival qualifier "of holiness" ($\dot{\alpha}\gamma\iota\omega\sigma\acute{\upsilon}\nu\eta\varsigma$), maintaining that it has been used expressly to show that the Holy Spirit is not in view.[78] Admittedly this is a unique combination, not occurring elsewhere in the New Testament, other early Christian literature, or the Septuagint. However, this hardly means that the Holy Spirit is not being described, or that it refers to Christ's divine nature. As a matter of fact, the slight linguistic evidence available decidedly favors a reference to the Holy Spirit. (i) The most plausible explanation is that it is a Hebrism, an exact rendering of רוּחַ קָדְשׁוֹ.[79] This expression occurs three times in the Old Testament, referring to

---

76. An exception on the view that the two natures are being contrasted is Calvin, who finds a reference to the Holy Spirit. However; in maintaining at the same time that "flesh" (v. 3) refers to Christ's human nature, he destroys the parallelism. This criticism is made by Hodge, *Romans*, p. 28.

77. The older liberal interpretation did see in these verses a contrast between the two elements of Christ's common humanity, e.g., W. Sanday and A. C. Headlam, *A Critical and Exegetical Commentary on the Epistle to the Romans*, ICC (New York: Charles Scribner's Sons, 1896), p. 7; E. Kühl, *Der Brief des Paulus an die Römer* (Leipzig: Quelle & Meyer, 1913), p. 10. The insuperable problem with this view, however, is that it is difficult to see how the resurrection, specifically bodily in character, can be associated positively with the noncorporeal aspect of Christ's person in explicit antithesis to the corporeal aspect (cf. Warfield, "Paul's Christ," p. 246).

78. Hodge, *Romans*, p. 28; Warfield, "Paul's Christ," p. 249.

79. O. Procksch, *TDNT*, 1:114.

that which indwells the faithful and is capable of grief. Moreover, in each instance the Septuagint translates it with πνεῦμα ἅγιον (Ps. 50:11; Isa. 63:10f.). (ii) One other occurrence of this expression is extant, in The Testaments of the Twelve Patriarchs.[80] Here too the πνεῦμα in view is that which rests upon "the saints" (with which they are anointed?).[81]

If anything, then, linguistic considerations support the analogy of Paul's usage which favors a reference here to the Holy Spirit. This reference is further corroborated by the correlation of πνεῦμα and the resurrection through the two prepositional phrases which both describe the action of the participle "declared." This points to the activity of the Holy Spirit in the resurrection, which occupies such a prominent place in Paul's thinking.[82]

(b) Another major difficulty is that the view of Hodge and Warfield sees the significance of the resurrection in these verses to be its noetic function with reference to Christ's divine nature, in making evident his divinity. Such a notion is not only not present elsewhere in Paul but is clearly foreign to the central thrust of his teaching.[83] The resurrection of Christ is the resurrection of the firstfruits, the firstborn, the second Adam. It has no meaning apart from the solidarity between Christ and believers, apart from what he has in common with them. With reference to Christ's person, for Paul the resurrec-

---

80. The origin of this pseudepigraphon has been a matter of some controversy. R. H. Charles, *The Greek Versions of the Testaments of the Twelve Patriarchs* (Oxford: Clarendon Press, 1908), held to a Hebrew original written at the close of the second century B.C. (p. ix), and a first Greek version dating before A.D. 50 and quoted in Rom. 1:32 and I Thess. 2:16 (pp. xliiif.). The prevailing thesis at present, in one form or other, is that it is a Christian redaction of a Jewish writing (itself embodying several layers of transmission) and dates from the second century; see J. Becker, *Untersuchungen zur Entstehungsgeschichte der Testamente der zwölf Patriarchen* (Leiden: E. J. Brill, 1970), pp. 376f.; cf. F.-M. Braun, "Les Testaments des XII Patriarches et le problème de leur origine," *Revue Biblique*, 67(1960):516ff.

81. "And he [the new priest] shall give to the saints to eat from the tree of life, and the spirit of holiness (πνεῦμα ἁγιωσύνης) shall be on them" (Testament of Levi 18:11; Charles, *Greek Versions*, p. 64).

82. Those who see a reference to the Holy Spirit assess the precise force of "holiness" differently: Vos considers it a designation of God (the Father?) in his specific deity in sharp contrast to David ("Eschatology and the Spirit," p. 230); Ridderbos views it as accentuating the divinity of the Spirit (*Romeinen*, p. 25); Murray makes no attempt to explain it, finding a reference to the Spirit beyond question on the basis of his close conjunction with the resurrection (*Romans*, 1:11); cf. H. Lietzmann, *An die Römer*, Handbuch zum Neuen Testament, 8, 4th ed. (Tübingen: J. C. B. Mohr, 1933), p. 25.

83. See above, p. 65.

tion concerns his human nature, not his divine nature.[84]
Moreover, as such, its significance is not purely noetic.
For as I Cor. 15:45 and II Cor. 3:17 make clear, the resurrection produces a real transformation in the person of
Christ, a change which is analogous to that experienced
by believers (cf. esp. I Cor. 15:51 with vv. 45ff.). Christ's
resurrection is not evidential with respect to his divinity
but transforming with respect to his humanity.

   (c) Inasmuch as syntactical lines put verses 3 and 4
within the orbit of "gospel" (v. 1), they function as a capsule statement of the gospel, a summary declaration of
"the Christ that Paul preached," to employ Warfield's
own language. Indeed, Warfield has given this point its
most forceful emphasis.[85] But how appropriate for this
purpose is a reference to the two natures? The two-
natured person of Christ is certainly an indispensable
aspect of gospel proclamation. As we will see, it is
definitely present in these clauses. But it is not the gospel
in a nutshell. The doctrine of Christ's two natures
coupled with nothing more than "incidental," "accidental," "indifferent" (Warfield) reference to his history and
work is *not* "the power of God unto salvation" (v. 16).
While this objection can be pressed too far, its force must
be appreciated and an effort made to discover whether
some other interpretation fits the context better. As a matter of fact, the brunt of all three objections here to the two
natures interpretation is that, despite its apparent
plausibility and cogency, it fails to find a place within the
broader context of Paul's theology.

   (3) A proper interpretation of these verses must appreciate the centrality of the temporal factor minimized
by Warfield. This can be seen by carefully tracing Paul's
progression of thought. The subject of both participial
clauses is "his Son" (v. 3a). While conceivably "Son" is
used proleptically, anticipating what the subject becomes
by virtue of the events described in the succeeding

84. Cf. Murray (*Romans*, 1:11), who stresses that the resurrection, "it must not be
forgotten, concerns Christ's human nature—only in respect of his human nature
was he raised from the dead."
85. "In doing this [Paul] is led to describe briefly the Gospel which had been committed
to him, and that particularly with regard to its contents." Here is "one of the chief
sources of our knowledge of Paul's conception of Christ." "Nowhere else do we get a
more direct description of specifically the Christ that Paul preached." ("Paul's Christ,"
pp. 236, 237; cf. pp. 238, 239, 252).

clauses, more natural is a reference to the Son's specific identity in what follows, that is, a reference to the subject's relationship to God (cf. v. 1), antecedent to and independent of the experiences described. Apparently, then, preexistent, eternal sonship is in view.

Elsewhere Paul says that God sent (did not spare) his (own) Son (Rom. 8:3, 32; Gal. 4:4). Although in Romans 8:32 the proximate reference may be to the death of Christ, in the light of verse 3 the manifestation and sufferings leading to that death are in view implicitly. In each case, then, Christ is sent (in the likeness of sinful flesh, born of a woman), not spared, that is, incarnated, in his specific identity as the Son.[86] This teaching, coupled with the fact that Paul considers Christ to be divine (Phil. 2:6; cf. Rom. 9:5), shows conclusively that the subject of Romans 1:3a is the preexistent, divine Son of God,[87] and that the divinity of Christ is already present at this point, prior to what is said in either of the following clauses.

The basic thrust of verse 3, then, is that the preexistent Son of God became a man. In other words, the theanthropic constitution of Christ's person is fully present before verse 4. The incarnation is adequately described by "born of the seed of David." This raises the question of the function of "according to the 'flesh'" ($\kappa\alpha\tau\grave{\alpha}$ $\sigma\acute{\alpha}\rho\kappa\alpha$). Does it in a purely epexegetical fashion make the assumption of human nature explicit? Or does it contribute something additional? Does the reference of $\sigma\acute{\alpha}\rho\xi$ include more than Christ's human nature?[88] A brief exploration of Paul's use of $\sigma\acute{\alpha}\rho\xi$ is necessary to answer this question.

The hallmark of Paul's use of $\sigma\acute{\alpha}\rho\xi$ is its complexity.[89]

---

86. Note the emphatic forms ($\dot{\epsilon}\alpha\upsilon\tau\acute{o}\nu$, $\dot{\iota}\delta\acute{\iota}o\upsilon$) employed in Rom. 8: 3, 32.

87. Cf. Murray, *Romans*, 1:5f; Kramer, *Christ, Lord, Son of God*, pp. 111-123.

88. Neither Hodge nor Warfield asks this question. Instead they make the uninvestigated assumption that the reference is to Christ's human nature, one of the fundamental supports of their interpretation. A similar failing mars the exegesis of Murray, who likewise finds a reference to human nature (*Romans*, 1:8), although he sees correctly that the basic contrast is between successive stages and that $\pi\nu\epsilon\hat{\upsilon}\mu\alpha$ in verse 4 refers to the Holy Spirit. Despite his remarks to circumvent the difficulty (pp. 10f.), this last point can only be held inconsistently and is vulnerable to the criticism Hodge and Warfield would bring: it destroys the parallelism.

89. No aspect of Paul's anthropology has received more attention in recent decades. Cf. with the following discussion esp. Bultmann, *Theology*, 1:232-239 and Ridderbos, *Paul*, pp. 64-68; cf. also E. Schweizer, *TDNT*, 7:125-138; R. Jewett, *Paul's Anthropological Terms* (Leiden: E. J. Brill, 1971), pp. 49-166, 453-456.

Still, it is possible to distinguish three basic meanings. In the first place, σάρξ (as synonymous with σῶμα) refers to materiality, including the material aspect of man, his corporeality (e.g., II Cor. 4:11; Gal. 4:13f.; Col. 1:22, with reference to Christ). This usage corresponds to the preponderant meaning of the English "flesh" but is the least frequent in Paul. In the second place, against the background of Old Testament usage, σάρξ can mean the whole person, man in his entirety (e.g., Rom. 3:20; I Cor. 1:29; Gal. 2:16). The word is an index, a synonym, for what is specifically human. An extension of this usage is its collective force indicating genetic connection and racial solidarity (Rom. 11:14).

A third, even broader meaning, virtually overlooked until recently, is the most prominent in Paul. It has what is best described as an atmospheric quality. The term refers to the sphere of human existence, man's environment, the natural, earthly order with all that is characteristic of human life and necessary for its maintenance. It brings into view a comprehensive state of affairs, a world order. Pointedly, and this is basic to the whole of Paul's theology, σάρξ in this sense is intensionally synonymous with αἰών, to be precise, this (old) age (οὗτος ὁ αἰών).[90]

This atmospheric, "aeonic" meaning is found primarily in the distinctively Pauline phrases ἐν σαρκί (e.g., Rom. 7:5; II Cor. 10:3; Gal. 2:20; Philemon 16) and κατὰ σάρκα (e.g., I Cor. 1:26; Gal. 4:23; Eph. 6:5). So, for example, in Ephesians 6:5 where slaves are commanded to obey their masters κατὰ σάρκα, Paul is not reflecting on bondage characterized by some familial or racial tie but on a relationship marking the present order of things, this age. Even clearer is the pattern of usage in I Corinthians 1:20ff.: The wise man, the debater of this age, taken up with the wisdom of the world (v. 20), that is, the wisdom of this age (2:6; cf. 3:18, 19), is none other than the wise man κατὰ σάρκα (v. 26).[91]

90. Cf. Vos, "Eschatology and the Spirit," p. 255, n. 61: "It [σάρξ] is an organism, an order of things beyond the individual man, even beyond human nature.
91. In Gal. 2:20 ("that which I now live ἐν σαρκί . . .") Paul is probably not referring simply to his individual bodily life. Rather his point is that as he continues to exist in the old aeon, he lives by faith. This verse illustrates why it is sometimes difficult to grasp the exact meaning of Paul's usage. For it is exactly in the somatic aspect of personal existence, that is, as our bodies are subject to corruption and death (I Cor. 15:42ff.), that our continuing existence in the old aeon (ἐν σαρκί) becomes painfully evident.

I Corinthians 1:20ff. also illustrates the depreciatory, ethically negative sense Paul's use of σάρξ often has. The wise man κατὰ σάρκα is opposed in his wisdom to the wisdom of God (v. 21) and considers the preaching of the gospel foolishness (v. 23). Even more sharply in Romans 8:4ff., those who are ἐν σαρκί are not able to please God (v. 8). The mind of the σάρξ, hostile toward God (v. 7), is death (v. 6). According to Galatians 5:19ff. different vices are the works of the σάρξ.[92] There is, however, nothing inhering in the term σάρξ itself (in whatever sense) that explains why Paul views it as the source of sin and death. Rather, here as elsewhere his historical perspective is essential. Because of the disobedience of Adam the old aeon has become corrupt, the order of the first Adam has become the order of death, that is, the σάρξ has *become* weak.

Both the "aeonic" and at times ethically qualified uses of σάρξ reveal the full dimensions of the antithesis with πνεῦμα. The ethical nature of this contrast is apparent in passages like Romans 8:4ff. and Galatians 5:12ff. Nor is it difficult to see that the "enveloping," "circumambient," "atmospheric"[93] quality of the Spirit's working characterizes the antithesis as a whole. I Corinthians 15:42-49, for instance, contrasts the new, eschatological creation, begun at Christ's resurrection and distinguished as "spiritual," with the old order described as "psychical" (ψυχικόν, see esp. v. 46). This comprehensive contrast is a variant of the πνεῦμα-σάρξ antithesis. For the body of the present order, set over against the body of the final, resurrection order, is characterized by corruption, dishonor and weakness (vv. 42f.), things regularly associated with the σάρξ and contrasted with the Spirit.[94] Further, the adjective ψυχικός, employed with a comprehensive, summarizing force (vv. 44, 46), is in its only other occurrence clearly synonymous with σάρκινος and σαρκικός (cf. I Cor. 2:14 with 3:1, 3) as the latter are also contrasted pointedly with πνευματικός (3:1). To generalize, σάρξ describes the self-maintaining impetus of the present evil age, better, it focuses the inertia and weakness of the old

92. The fact that Paul includes enmities, jealousy, and envyings in his list shows how little he considers the material aspect of man's person a producing cause.
93. Vos, *Eschatology*, p. 59. Cf. above, p. 73.
94. See the discussion and verses cited above, p. 70.

aeon[95] in antithesis to the Spirit as the power of the age-to-come (cf. Heb. 6:5).

The πνεῦμα-σάρξ antithesis, then, while it has important anthropological implications, is fundamentally a historical contrast.[96] Intrinsic to it is what Warfield dismisses in passing,[97] the capacity for expressing temporal distinction. It is an antithesis between two aeons, one present and one coming, between the old world order which is passing away and the new which remains (II Cor. 4:18; cf. I Cor. 7:31). While this "aeonic," eschatological dimension is largely beneath the surface of the text, several other examples make plain its pervasive and controlling place in Paul's thinking. In Romans 12:2 the renewing work of the Holy Spirit (cf. Titus 3:5) is not contrasted with conformity to the σάρξ, as might be expected, but with conformity to "this age." According to I Corinthians 2:6ff. spiritual wisdom (cf. vv. 10ff.) is opposed not to the sarkic wisdom spoken of elsewhere (II Cor. 1:12) but to the wisdom of this age (v. 6) and the knowledge and ways of the rulers of this age (v. 8). Again, in II Corinthians 4:4 Satan as "the god of this age," blinds men to the glory of Christ, who is the Spirit (3:17), central to the eschatological order (3:6ff.).

Finally, not every association of σάρξ with an individual need involve attributing to him its evil, sinful predicates. This is perhaps clearest in II Corinthians 10:3 where Paul says that although he lives ἐν σαρκί, he does not conform to its norms and standards (κατὰ σάρκα; cf. Gal. 2:20). Also, apart from Romans 1:3 are those instances where σάρξ is used with reference to Christ (e.g., Rom. 9:5; Eph. 2:14; I Tim. 3:16).

This survey of Paul's use of σάρξ was prompted by the question whether in Romans 1:3 κατὰ σάρκα refers to more than Christ's individual human nature. That question can now be answered affirmatively. The phrase brings into view not only Christ's human nature but also and pointedly the order into which the assumption of humanity brought him, the environment with which this humanity is necessarily associated and from which it can-

95. Cf. Vos, *Eschatology*, p. 300.
96. "With Paul, both in regard to the σάρξ and the πνεῦμα, the historical facto remains the controlling one" (Vos, Eschatology and the Spirit," p. 246).
97. "Paul's Christ," pp. 244f.; see above, p. 102f.

not be abstracted. The full thought of verse 3 is that by in-carnation (by being born of the seed of David) the eternal Son of God entered the sphere of σάρξ, the old aeon, the present evil age; his personal, incarnate mode of ex-istence was conformed to the sarkic world-order entered at birth. Grammatically, both prepositional phrases are adverbial, describing the act of incarnation, but in the case of κατὰ σάρκα it is employed "so as to throw em-phasis on the result rather than on the initial act."[98]

The pattern of thought in verse 4 if the same: by[99] resurrection the preexistent Son, having become in-carnate in the old order (the subject as defined in v. 3), en-tered the sphere of the Spirit, the new aeon, the coming age; his personal, incarnate mode of existence is now con-formed to the pneumatic world-order entered at the resur-rection. Again, the latter two prepositional phrases, corresponding to their parallels in verse 3, are adverbial. This confirms the instrumentality of the Spirit in raising Jesus, intimated in Romans 8:11 and elsewhere. But κατά, paralleling its use in verse 3, also brings into view the re-sultant state in its specifically spiritual character.

Verse 4, then, is of a piece with I Corinthians 15:45 and II Corinthians 3:17. Here as there the Holy Spirit so thoroughly transforms Christ at his resurrection that in comparison to what went before he now exists "according to the Spirit." In this instance, too, the resurrection is crucial to what Christ is and continues to be. While here the resurrected Christ is described not as (life-giving) Spirit but as "Son of God in power,"[100] the two

---

98. Vos, "Eschatology and the Spirit," p. 229; cf. Sokolowski, *Geist und Leben*, p. 57.

99. The force of the preposition, while not fully causal, is, in view of the nature of the resurrection, certainly more than temporal. The comment of M.-J. Lagrange can hardly be improved upon: "Accordingly, ἐξ indicates less than causality and more than posteriority, a well-suited concomitance." (*Épitre aux Romans* [Paris: J. Gabalda, 1950],p. 8).

100. Most probably "in power" is used attributively (so Michel, *an die Römer*, p. 32; Murray, *Romans*, 1:9, n. 9; Ridderbos, *Romeinen*, p. 26). Several factors favor this conclusion: (1) As verse 3a shows, sonship not in the absolute but as a newly qualified phase is in view in verse 4. (2) In the contrast, emphasis is on resultant states rather than initial acts. (3) In the parallelism, "Son of God" and "in power" have no counterparts, and so are closely associated as a unit required to fill out the meaning of "declared." II Cor. 13:4, which Sanday and Headlam (*Romans*, p. 9) appeal to as determining an adverbial connection, is quite compatible with an at-tributive rendering. The emphasis there as here is not so much on the act of resur-rection as the ongoing life of the resurrected Christ.

designations have a close affinity in Paul's world of thought where (redemptive) δύναμις is always a pointedly pneumatic category.[101] The Spirit invested with power is the one who makes alive.

There is, however, an important new element introduced here. Verse 4 teaches that at the resurrection Christ began a new and unprecedented phase of divine sonship. The eternal Son of God, who was born, lived, and died κατὰ σάρκα, has been raised κατὰ πνεῦμα and so, in his messianic identity (of the seed of David), has become what he was not before: the Son of God in power.[102] This pneumatic sonship of Christ will not concern us further here, except to point out that in the light of it, the view of Hodge and Warfield that "Son of God" is "not a term of office, nor expressive of any relation assumed in time,"[103] is in need of such qualification that it no longer serves the purpose of their argument.[104]

As in I Corinthians 15:45 so here too the personal significance of the resurrection for Jesus is set in the same notably broader context. The πνεῦμα-σάρξ antithesis brings into view nothing less than the contrast between the two ages,[105] involving the conclusion that the eschatological aeon begins with Christ's resurrection. This conclusion is confirmed by the easily-overlooked composition of the phrase ἐξ ἀναστάσεως νεκρῶν (both substantives are anarthrous, without pronominal qualification of the first or repetition of the preposition before the second). This combination (cf. Acts 26:23) is best explained by Paul's desire to introduce the idea of resurrection in a more general, qualitative way, contrasted with birth in a broad, generic fashion: As birth is characteristic of the old aeon,

---

101. See above, p. 68f.

102. "From resurrection-beginnings, from an eschatological genesis dated the pneumatic state of Christ's glory which is described as sonship of God ἐν δυνάμει" (Vos, "Eschatology and the Spirit," p. 230).

103. Hodge, *Romans*, p. 25.

104. The identification of the subject in verse 3a excludes an adoptionistic christology here. For the widespread view that Paul is modifying an originally adoptionistic formulation see, e.g., Schweizer, *TDNT*, 6:417; Kramer, *Christ, Lord, Son of God*, pp. 110f.; cf. Michel, *an die Römer*, p. 32. For a trenchant criticism and rejection of attempts to find adoptionism here as well as elsewhere in the New Testament, cf. G. Sevenster, *Die Christologie van het Nieuwe Testament*, 2nd ed., (Amsterdam: Uitgeversmaatschappij, 1948), pp. 201-203, 309-312, 341-343.

105. Vos, "Eschatology and the Spirit," p. 230. Cf. A. Nygren, *Commentary on Romans*, trans. C. C. Rasmussen (Philadelphia: Muhlenburg Press, 1949), pp. 53f.

the sarkic world, so resurrection marks the beginning of the new aeon, the eschatological, pneumatic world.[106] Verse 4 expresses the central theme of Paul's resurrection theology: the epochal character of Christ's resurrection. His resurrection forms a unity with the resurrection of believers; his resurrection is the "firstfruits."[107]

Conclusion: Romans 1:3 and 4 do not contrast two co-existing aspects (the two natures) in the make-up of Christ's person. The insuperable obstacles for this view are the "aeonic" nature of the πνεῦμα-σάρξ antithesis and the economic rather than purely ontological character of the designation "Son of God" (v. 4). Instead, the contrast is between two successive phases in Christ's history, implying two successive modes of *incarnate* existence. The contrast is antithetic and progressive, in the language of dogmatics, a contrast between the states of humiliation and exaltation. The same basic pattern of thought is found elsewhere in Paul, notably in Philippians 2:6-11 and I Timothy 3:16 (cf. I Peter 3:18).

This interpretation passes the test at those points where the view of Hodge and Warfield was found wanting.[108] (1) It refers πνεῦμα (v. 4) to the Holy Spirit and so, while maintaining the parallel, does justice to the πνεῦμα-σάρξ contrast without having to find an exception to Paul's regular and distinctive use of it. (2) It finds the significance of the resurrection (v. 4) to lie specifically in what Christ is as incarnate and in solidarity with his people, again conforming to the invariable pattern of Paul's teaching elsewhere. (3) It meets the requirement of the immediate context that

---

106. If the reference were to Christ's resurrection as a single event, one would expect something like ἐξ ἀναστάσεως αὐτοῦ ἐκ νεκρῶν. Among the commentators, Nygren especially has stressed this point (*Romans*, pp. 48-52); cf. Vos, "Eschatology and the Spirit," p. 230: "Paul is not thinking of *the* resurrection of Christ as an event, but of what happened to Christ in its generic qualitative capacity, as an epoch partaking of a strictly eschatological nature."

107. It is not warranted to find in these verses a denial of either the virgin birth or the bestowal of the Spirit upon Christ at his baptism. "Precisely, because he speaks of the pneumatic state in the absolute eschatological sense, he could disregard in this connection, the twofold supernatural equipment just named, for the reason that it did not give rise to a state ἐν δυνάμει κατὰ πνεῦμα such as characterizes the life of the risen Christ." Moreover, in verse 4 "the emphasis rests not on the initial act of the resurrection but on the resulting state. In regard to the act as such Paul would not have denied that the entrance of Jesus upon the σάρξ was likewise κατὰ πνεῦμα" (Vos, "Eschatology and the Spirit," p. 231, n. 27).

108. Cf. above, pp. 103-105.

these clauses provide a capsule summary of the gospel. For the *history* of Christ is the gospel in a nutshell. Not Christ the God-man, but Christ, the eternal Son of God become incarnate in the present evil age with the humiliation, suffering, and death this sarkic existence involved, and as the incarnate Son of God raised up to be the source for others of the eschatological power and life this pneumatic existence of the coming age involves—this is the gospel to which Paul goes on to give such unsurpassed development in the body of Romans.[109]

Acts 13:33

The close connection in thought between Romans 1:4 and Acts 13:33 emerges when the precise reference of the participle "raising" ($\dot{\alpha}\nu\alpha\sigma\tau\dot{\eta}\sigma\alpha\varsigma$) in the latter is clarified. The commentators differ widely on this point: is it the incarnation,[110] Jesus' baptism, [111] his resurrection,[112] or his earthly appearance in general?[113]

No convincing argument exists against a specific reference to the resurrection. The primary objection usually raised is that the unmistakable reference to the resurrection in the following verse requires verse 33 to have a broader sense or to refer to some other event.[114] This reasoning, however, is offset by other contextual considerations: (1) In the structure of Paul's sermon, which begins at verse 16, verse 30 is a distinct point of transition, introducing a section (through v. 37) bracketed by brief but emphatic assertions of the resurrection. Accordingly, the intervening verses explicate the

109. Cf. Greijdanus, *Romeinen*, p. 61: "The gospel as such is not simply that He became man, has two natures, and reigns in glory, but that He came from David's seed $\kappa\alpha\tau\dot{\alpha}\ \sigma\dot{\alpha}\rho\kappa\alpha$, bearing the punishment of our sins and for our redemption, and in connection with this was clothed with divine majesty and given supreme authority—that is the message of salvation, which Paul also preached and which is expressed here."

110. E.g., J. A. Alexander, *The Acts of the Apostles*, 3rd ed. (Philadelphia: Presbyterian Board of Publication, 1857), 2:29.

111. F. F. Bruce, *Commentary on the Book of Acts*, NICNT (Grand Rapids: Eerdmans, 1956), pp. 275f.

112. E.g., E. Haenchen, *The Acts of the Apostles*, trans. B. Noble and G. Shinn (Philadelphia: Westminster Press, 1971), p. 411; cf. Murray, "Who Raised Up Jesus," p. 117, n. 2.

113. J. Calvin, *The Acts of the Apostles*, trans. J. W. Fraser and W. J. G. McDonald (Grand Rapids: Eerdmans, 1965), 1:377; F. W. Grosheide, *De Handelingen der Apostelen*, KNT (Amsterdam: H. A. Van Bottenberg, 1942), 1:431. Both maintain, however, that with this broader reference the resurrection is most directly in view.

114. So Alexander, Bruce, Grosheide.

significance of the resurrection. (2) The pattern of the sermon is such that the "raising" of Jesus in the sense of his
birth and ministry is already present in verses 23-25,
followed in sequence by his condemnation, death (vv.
27-29), and resurrection (vv. 30ff.). (3) In the immediate
context verse 34 does not simply mention the resurrection
but introduces the *additional* thought, developed in the
succeeding verses, that the resurrected one will not undergo decay; here verse 34 is best understood as building
on a reference to the resurrection in the preceding verse
Verse 33, then, most likely refers specifically to Jesus'
resurrection, as promised in Psalm 2:7 (cf. Heb. 1:5; 5:5).

The exact meaning of this verse depends on the
relationship of the two clauses in the quotation of Psalm
2:7. Does "my Son" in the first clause describe the object
of the action in the second clause (begetting) in the identity in which he underwent this action or in his identity as
a result of this action? In other words, is the designation
"Son" in the first clause ontological or messianic? This
question may be left open here, for with either option the
thought is much the same and close to Romans 1:4.[115] In
the one case, corresponding to the tie between Romans
1:3a and 4, the thought would be that the eternal Son entered on a new phase of sonship at the resurrection. In the
latter alternative the thought would fall entirely within
the orbit of Romans 1:4 and involve an explicit application of the title "Son" on the basis of the resurrection.
Both possibilities, however, clearly express the constitutive, generative (an element present in Rom. 1:4 by
virtue of the contrast with "born," v. 3) significance of the
resurrection for Christ *as Son.*

The Resurrection as the Redemption of Christ

In calling the resurrection Christ's redemption,
"redemption" is being employed in a broader sense,
similar to the wider of the two primary meanings it has in
dogmatic usage, indicating deliverance or salvation. This,
as a matter of fact, is frequently the force of Paul's use of
$\dot{\alpha}\pi o\lambda\acute{\nu}\tau\rho\omega\sigma\iota\varsigma$ (Rom. 8:23; I Cor. 1:30; Eph. 1:14; 4:30).

---

115. The pattern of thought in Psalm 89:26, 27 supports the former alternative, II
Samuel 7:14 the latter. The use of Psalm 2:7 elsewhere in the New Testament
(Heb. 1:5; 5:5) does not settle the question.

However, the term also has the more specific meaning of a ransom-price and in this sense is repeatedly applied to Jesus' death (Rom. 3:24f.; I Cor. 6:20; 7:23; Gal. 3:13; 4:5; Eph. 1:7; I Tim. 2:6; Titus 2:14).[116]

These observations prompt at this point some preliminary remarks concerning the fundamental question of the relationship of Christ's resurrection to his death. No one will dispute that Paul never divorces the one from the other, nor that for him each is meaningless without the other. Especially applicable to his writings is the observation of Calvin that in the New Testament, references to the death alone or to the resurrection alone cover each other in a synecdochic fashion.[117] Inseparability, however, is not indistinguishability. Plainly Paul thinks of Christ's death and the resurrection as different events on the same plane of historical occurrence. The resurrection is not an aspect or component part of the death.[118] Rather, as Calvin's statement itself reflects, each has a meaning of its own, which is suppressed at the risk of seriously distorting Paul's gospel.

As we have already tried to show, the significance of the resurrection is more than noetic, it involves more than an unveiling of the efficacy of the cross.[119] What now needs to be stressed is that in Paul's world of thought the death of Jesus as a discrete experience is *not* given positive or constructive import. This is not to question that Paul confessed with the rest of the early Christian community that it was impossible for Jesus to be held in the power of

---

116. On these points cf. esp. B. B. Warfield, "The New Testament Terminology of 'Redemption,' " *Biblical Doctrines* (New York: Oxford University Press, 1929), pp. 352-366; L. Morris; *The Apostolic Preaching of the Cross* (Grand Rapids: Eerdmans, 1956), pp. 26-56.

117. "So then, let us remember that whenever mention is made of his death alone, we are to understand at the same time what belongs to his resurrection. Also, the same synecdoche applies to the word 'resurrection': whenever it is mentioned separately from death, we are to understand it as including what has to do especially with his death" (J. Calvin, *Institutes of the Christian Religion*, 2:16:13, trans. J. T. McNeill, The Library of Christian Classics, 20 [Philadelphia, The Westminster Press, 1960], 1:521).

118. Such a reduction of the resurrection is, e.g., the thesis developed in a massive fashion by E. Güttgemanns, *Der leidende Apostel und sein Herr. Studien zur paulinischen Christologie*, Forschungen zur Religion und Literatur des Alten und Neuen Testaments, 90, (Göttingen: Vandenhoeck & Ruprecht, 1966); cf. esp. pp. 247-281.

119. Cf. also the discussion of Berkouwer, *The Work of Christ*, pp. 189-193.

death (Acts 2:24) or that he died, "the just for the unjust" (I Peter 3:18). But in all that is unique about Christ's death (cf. esp. Phil. 2:6-8), nothing is more fundamental than its adamic significance; it is the death of the second Adam (cf. esp. Rom. 5:18f.). It is not properly understood other than as the death of him who, knowing no sin, was made sin (II Cor. 5:21). Everything Paul teaches about the death of others applies, *mutatis mutandis*, in the light of Romans 8:3, to the death of Christ. His death is the wages of the sin he became (cf. Rom. 6:23), and the state of death he endured for a time is the nadir of his exposure to the wrath of the Father. Nothing resident in Jesus' death, as death, relaxes its severity or alleviates its grimness.

It is, then, not only meaningful but necessary to speak of the resurrection as the redemption of Christ. The resurrection is nothing if not his deliverance from the power and curse of death which was in force until the moment of being raised. Here too the adamic factor is pivotal. The resurrection is the salvation of Jesus as the last Adam; it and no other event in his experience is the point of *his* transition from wrath to grace. This does not at all imply that Paul compromises the absolute necessity and intrinsic efficacy of Christ's death (as an atonement). It does mean, however, that he does not confuse the ransom price, no matter how sublime and precious, with what is secured by its payment. To Paul's way of thinking, as long as Christ remains dead, Satan and sin are triumphant,[120] or, more broadly, the dominion of the old aeon remains unbroken. Strictly speaking, not Christ's death, but his resurrection (that is, his exaltation) marks the completion of the once-for-all accomplishment of redemption. Accordingly, in a verse like Romans 6:10 ("the death that he died, he died to sin . . .") it is essential to distinguish carefully between his death as the act of dying to sin and the resultant condition of being dead to sin. The latter, as the preceding verse makes clear, is exponential of his *resurrected* state in which death is no longer master over him. In fact, only by virtue of his resurrection is his death

---

120. "No matter how he emphasizes the significance of the cross, *without Christ's resurrection* there would still be condemnation because sin would still be supreme" (Berkouwer, *Work*, p. 190; italics in the Dutch original); cf. Murray, *Romans*, 1:9.

a dying to sin. A soteriology structured so that it moves directly from the death of Christ to the application to others of the benefits purchased by that death, substantially short-circuits Paul's own point of view. For him the accomplishment of redemption is only first definitively realized in the application to Christ himself (by the Father through the Spirit) at the resurrection of the benefits purchased by his own obedience unto death.

These general reflections prompt further inquiry into how precisely the principal categories Paul uses to explicate the application of redemption to the individual believer are related to Christ's resurrection as the redemption of the last Adam. While Paul does not address this question explicitly, his discussion does bear on its answer, and contains important structural elements of his soteriology as a whole.

Adoption

In the discussion of Romans 1:3, 4 above one point passed over is the use of the participle ὁρισθέντος in verse 4. In the parallelism of the two verses it is hardly the natural, anticipated counterpart of "born" (γενομένου, v. 3). This suggests that it functions to bring out a noteworthy aspect of the resurrection not otherwise apparent. What, then, is the meaning of the verb ὁρίζω used here to describe the resurrection?

It has been customary in translating this verb here to force a decision between "declare" and "appoint." The former was chosen by most of the older commentators.[121] This, however, rested almost entirely on the conviction that "Son of God" has exclusively ontological significance and therefore cannot describe what Christ is by virtue of an installation or appointment. More recent interpretation, recognizing this title to be a messianic designation of exaltation, has adopted the latter alternative.[122] Besides fitting well here, this is the uniform meaning of the word elsewhere in the New Testament (Luke 22:22; Acts 2:23; 10:42; 11:29; 17:26, 31; Heb. 4:7). Still, a declarative force is difficult to eliminate entirely, being close to, if not involved in, the idea of appointment itself

---

121. E.g., Calvin, *Romans*, p. 16; Hodge, *Romans*, pp. 26f.
122. E.g., Vos, "Eschatology and the Spirit," p. 229; Michel, *an die Römer*, p. 32; Ridderbos, *Romeinen*, p. 26; Murray, *Romans*, 1:9.

and present in the notion of decree virtually presupposed by this verb.[123] Also in some instances its meaning is plainly declaratory.[124] Consequently, while the thought of effectual appointment is prominent, a declarative nuance is also present, so that in its effective, transforming character the resurrection has a declaratory significance. The resurrection is here viewed as a declaration which is constitutive in nature.[125] Moreover, this verb has an unmistakable juridical tone.[126] This suggests that the resurrection is a judicially constitutive declaration of sonship.[127] In other words, ὁρισθέντος underscores what is already intimated in recognizing that "Son of God" is a messianic designation: the resurrection of Jesus is his *adoption* (as the second Adam).

Virtually the same thought is found in Acts 13:33, if the first clause of the Psalm citation is to be taken messianically (cf. Heb. 1:5, 5:5). Also Philippians 2:6ff., leaving aside the complex discussion in recent decades about its origin, structure, and meaning, has the same basic pattern of thought found in Romans 1:3f.: preexistence (v. 6), humiliation (vv. 7-8), exaltation (vv. 9-11). The sweeping reference to the exaltation (v. 9) not only includes the resurrection, [128] but also suggests that the correlative giving of the name that is above every name is not an act additional to that described by the preceding verb but an important facet of the exaltation itself—an indication of the declarative, if not the adoptive, significance of the exaltation   (resurrection).[129]   Romans   8:23   pointedly

---

123. Cf. esp. Acts 2:23; also Paul's use of προορίζω (Rom. 8:29, 30; I Cor. 2:7; Eph. 1:5, 11).
124. For partial citation of this nonbiblical usage see Lietzmann, *an die Römer*, p. 25.
125. Cf. the comment of K. L. Schmidt (*TDNT*, 5:453): "The exegetical dispute whether R. 1:4, according to usage attested elsewhere, is a declaration or decree concerning Christ, or His appointment and institution to a function or relation etc., is not a matter of great urgency, since a divine declaration is the same as a divine appointment: God's *verbum* is *efficax.*"
126. This force is especially prominent in the Septuagint usage in Numbers 30:3ff. where both verb and noun (ὁρισμός) refer to a binding oath or an obligation entered into by a vow.
127. "Rom. 1:4 also mentions appointment as the 'Son,' fully corresponding to Old Testament-Jewish thinking, which considers sonship to be based on the legal act of appointment, not on the natural act of procreation" (Schweizer, *Erniedrigung und Erhöhung*, p. 137).
128. See above, pp. 91f.; cf. W. Hendriksen, *New Testament Commentary. Exposition of Philippians* (Grand Rapids: Baker Book House, 1967), p. 114.
129. Schweizer, *Erniedrigung*, p. 138.

describes the resurrection of believers as "adoption, the redemption of the body." The inherently forensic concept of adoption fulfills itself in the somatic transformation of resurrection, so that in view of the (Adamic) unity of the resurrection of Christ and believers, what is true of the latter holds for the former.

Justification

(1) According to I Timothy 3:16 Christ "was justified [vindicated] in the Spirit" (ἐδικαιώθη ἐν πνεύματι). The immediate context of this unusual expression demands at least a brief discussion. By now the virtually universal conclusion (even where the Pauline authorship of the letter is recognized) is that verse 16 is a pre-Pauline formulation.[130] Its presumably non-Pauline origin, however, as in the case of Romans 1:3f., does not make it any less properly his teaching, and, apart from some clearly offsetting factor, it ought to be interpreted by analogy with that teaching elsewhere.

In its context the verse is a self-contained unit consisting of six parallel lines, each beginning with a passive verb (with Christ the implied subject) followed by a single qualification, in all but one instance a prepositional phrase with ἐν. Various answers have been given to the question of internal structure. Preferable, in my judgment, is the view that there are three couplets; in each the two lines form an antithesis of their own expressing an aspect of the contrast brought into view by the verse as a whole and giving rise to the following chiastic pattern: ab/ba/ab.[131] In any case, the first two lines form a contrast: Christ's manifestation ἐν σαρκί is set over against his justification ἐν πνεύματι.

130. So, e.g., the more recent Reformed exegesis: C. Bouma, *De Brieven van den Apostel Paulus aan Timotheus en Titus*, KNT, 11 (Amsterdam: Van Bottenburg, 1942), p. 147; W. Hendriksen, *New Testament Commentary. Exposition of The Pastoral Epistles* (Grand Rapids: Baker House, 1957), p. 137; Ridderbos, *De Pastorale Brieven*, pp. 103f., pp. 106f.; cf. F. W. Grosheide, "De Heilige Geest in de brieven," *De Heilige Geest*, ed. J. H. Bavinck et al (Kampen: J. H. Kok, 1949), p. 112. Hendriksen and Ridderbos speak of a pre-Pauline hymn.

131. J. Jeremias, *Die Briefe an Timotheus und Titus*, NTD, 9, 8th ed. (Göttingen: Vandenhoeck & Ruprecht, 1963), p. 23; Ridderbos, *Brieven*, p. 104; cf. Schweizer, *Erniedrigung*, p. 63, n. 272; *TDNT*, 6:416f.; Hendriksen, *Pastorals*, p. 138. Cf. the qualifications of R. H. Gundry, "The Form, Meaning and Background of the Hymn Quoted in I Timothy 3:16," *Apostolic History and the Gospel*. F. F. Bruce Festschrift, ed. W. W. Gasque and R. P. Martin (Grand Rapids: Eerdmans, 1970), pp. 208f.

Not surprisingly, Calvin, Hodge, and others, recognizing the similarity with Romans 1:3b, see here a contrast between the humanity and divinity of Christ.[132] Some hold that the second line refers to Christ's vindication by endowment with the Holy Spirit during his earthly ministry (*despite* his manifestation in the "flesh").[133] Recent interpretation has increasingly maintained that the basic pattern is humiliation-exaltation with the second line referring primarily to the resurrection.[134]

This last viewpoint is almost certainly correct. What precisely, then, is the meaning of the second line? The answer seems to lie in the light of I Corinthians 15:42ff. and Romans 1:3f., giving the πνεῦμα-σάρξ antithesis here the same broad, aeonic scope it has there and elsewhere in Paul.[135] This fits the rest of the verse well. Scanning the nouns in the lines discloses the following pattern: flesh, nations, and world, on the one hand; Spirit, angels, and glory, on the other. In other words, the verse as a whole contrasts the earthly and heavenly orders.[136] Elsewhere for Paul this contrast as it centers in the experience of Christ, along with the antithesis between πνεῦμα and σάρξ, is an expression of the fundamental contrast between the two ages.[137] This spatial outlook is not a later hellenizing tendency threatening to supplant the temporal, two-age perspective,[138] but is based on the lat-

---

132. J. Calvin, *The Second Epistle of Paul the Apostle to the Corinthians and the Epistles to Timothy, Titus and Philemon*, trans. T. A. Smail (Grand Rapids: Eerdmans, 1964), pp. 233f.; Hodge, *Romans*, p. 28; P. Fairbairn, *The Pastoral Epistles* (Edinburgh: T. & T. Clark, 1874), p. 165; cf. J. N. D. Kelly, *The Pastoral Epistles*, Harper's New Testament Commentaries, ed. H. Chadwick (New York: Harper & Row, 1963), pp. 90f.

133. Grosheide, "Heilige Geest," p. 112; Hendriksen, *Pastorals*, p. 140. The latter includes the resurrection.

134. Bouma, *Brieven*, p. 149; Jeremias, *Briefe*, p. 24; Ridderbos, *Brieven*, p. 104; Schweizer, *Erniedrigung*, p. 64.

135. It seems to me that Gundry, in reaching the conclusion "that line 2 refers to the vindication of Christ during and by the *Descensus ad Inferos* in spirit-form between death and resurrection" ("Form," p. 213), has not done justice to this background.

136. Cf. Jeremias, *Briefe*, p. 23.

137. Cf. I Cor. 15:46ff. with 2:14f.; 3:1, 3; see above, p. 90.

138. So, e.g., E. Schweizer, "Two New Testament Creeds Compared," *Neotestamentica* (Zürich: Zwingli Verlag, 1963), p. 126: "This church thinks no more in a pattern of time and history. It is exclusively by images of space that she expresses her feelings, her problems and needs, as well as the answer which she found in Jesus Christ." Apart from other considerations, this conclusion (with reference to I Timothy 3:16) can only be drawn by ignoring the temporal element which is also present.

ter. It is a cosmic "dualism" resulting from the repatriation of (the incarnate) Christ into heaven through his resurrection and ascention.[139] The thought of the verse as a whole is, as in Romans 1:3f., progressive as well as antithetic, from humiliation to exaltation, that is, from old aeon to new, so that the first two lines in particular closely parallel, respectively, the two participial clauses in Romans 1:3f.

The second line, then, affirms that Christ's exaltation in the realm of the Spirit, the heavenly order, the new age, is his justification or vindication. Even if the prepositional phrase has a local rather than instrumental force, accenting the resultant state of exaltation, the resurrection is still regarded implicitly as Christ's justification or the point of entering into a state of being justified.[140] Nothing warrants a different sense for the verb than its virtually uniform meaning elsewhere in Paul. Its demonstrative force here is so close to the usual strictly declarative usage that a substantial difference in meaning can hardly be insisted upon.[141] The declarative significance of the resurrection in Romans 1:4 (cf. 8:23; Phil. 2:9) supports this indirectly. Certainly its use here is no less forensic, so that the translation "vindicated," if adopted to eliminate the usual forensic, declarative meaning, is wrong. How, then, does this statement relate to Paul's insistence that justification is the justification of the ungodly (Rom. 4:5)?

Once again the answer lies in the adamic nature of Christ's life, death, and resurrection. In becoming identified with his people Christ was made sin (II Cor. 5:21). At the very least this means that he bore the guilt of sin. Solidarity involved him in being treated as one ungodly, in becoming a curse (Gal. 3:13), in being made subject to the condemnation of the law (Gal. 4:5). The direct relevance of the resurrection on this guilt-bearing of the second Adam resides for Paul in the character of Christ's death as the penalty and seal of the condemnation he bore. As long as he remained in a state of death, the righteous character of his work, the efficacy of his obedience

---

139. Cf. Vos, *Eschatology*, pp. 40, 41; "Eschatology and the Spirit," pp. 245f.
140. Cf. the force of κατὰ πνεῦμα in Rom. 1:4 (see above, p. 110). Cf. also the contrast in I Peter 3:18: "put to death σαρκί, but made alive πνεύματι."
141. Cf. Murray, *Romans*, 1:351.

unto death remained in question, in fact, was implicitly denied. Consequently, the eradication of death in his resurrection is nothing less than the removal of the verdict of condemnation and the effective affirmation of his (adamic) righteousness. His resurrected state is the reward and seal which testifies perpetually to his perfect obedience.

> Christ's resurrection was the *de facto* declaration of God in regard to his being just. His quickening bears in itself the testimony of his justification. God through suspending the forces of death operating on Him, declared that the ultimate, the supreme consequence of sin had reached its termination. In other words, resurrection had annulled the sentence of condemnation.[142]

(2) According to Romans 4:25 Jesus was delivered up "for our sins" and was raised "for our justification."[143] Here our transgressions are associated with his death, giving the reason for it; our justification is associated with his resurrection, giving the reason for it. Debate over the meaning of this statement has revolved about the force of the preposition διά: is it causal (retrospective) or final (prospective)? While some have maintained that because of the parallelism of the clauses both occurrences must have the same force,[144] most commentators, failing to see why the parallelism must be pressed in this fashion,[145] consider it more natural to take the first preposition retrospectively, the second one prospectively.[146] The parallelism itself favors this rendering. These two clauses correspond closely to the pattern of thought in Romans 1:3f. and I Timothy 3:16, sharing as well a similar function with the former. As at the outset of the letter Paul gives a summary statement of the gospel, so here he states

---

142. Vos, *Eschatology*, p. 151; cf. "Eschatology and the Spirit," p. 236.

143. Somewhat paradoxically Marcus Bath considers this verse "the most enigmatic and the most instructive statement of Paul about the resurrection" (*Die Taufe—Ein Sakrament?* [Zollikon-Zürich: Evangelischer Verlag, 1951], p. 286).

144. So Vos, *Eschatology*, p. 151; Murray, *Romans*, 1:154.

145. Especially if, as is generally held, this verse is a pre-Pauline creedal formulation (e.g., Bultmann, *Theology*, 1:46f., 82; Michel, *an die Römer*, p. 111f.; C. K. Barrett, *A Commentary on the Epistle to the Romans*, Harper's New Testament Commentaries, ed. H. Chadwick, [New York: Harper & Brothers, 1957], pp. 99f.). Ridderbos (*Romeinen*, p. 104) is uncertain on this point; Kuss (*Römerbrief*, p. 195) insists that a non-Pauline origin cannot be proven.

146. E.g., Greijdanus, *Romeinen*, pp. 251f.; Ridderbos, *Romeinen*, p. 104; Michel, *an die Römer*, p. 112; Barrett, *Romans*, p. 100; Kuss, *Römerbrief*, p. 193.

in capsule form what is to be developed in the pivotal chapters (5—8) which immediately follow. Further, the parallelism is not only antithetic but progressive, so that here again we encounter a variation on the basic pattern of humiliation and exaltation. The prepositional phrases function within a single movement of thought: the first with respect to the one side of the process (humiliation), specifying its cause, the second with respect to the other side (exaltation), its outcome.

The end in view in Christ's resurrection, then, is our justification. How is this so? What, more exactly, is the relationship between the two? The answer lies in doing justice to the parallelism of the two clauses as a summary statement within the broader framework of Paul's teaching. Jesus' being delivered up (his death) on account of our transgressions identified him with us in the condemnation inevitably attendant on our transgressions; in fact his death is the pointed manifestation of this solidarity in condemnation. Consequently, his being raised on account of our justification identifies him with us in the justifying verdict inevitably attendant on the righteousness which he himself established for us (better, which he established for himself as he was one with us) by his obedience unto death; his resurrection is the pointed manifestation of this solidarity in justification. The unexpressed assumption is that Jesus' resurrection is his justification. His resurrection is his justification as the last Adam, the justification of the "firstfruits." This and nothing less is the bond between his resurrection and our justification.[147]

The same underlying assumption gives depth to what is on the surface in I Corinthians 15:17 (where in the im-

---

147. This point has largely been overlooked by the commentators. Murray (*Romans*, 1:156f.) gives perhaps the best discussion of the connection between Christ's resurrection and our justification. However, he does not draw the conclusion reached above, which underlies and unifies the five factors he does list. Jonathan Edwards (*Works* [New York: Leavitt & Allen, 1855], 4:95f.) saw that this verse teaches Christ's resurrection as his justification, and this conception has an important place in his own treatment of the doctrine of justification (cf. esp. pp. 66ff.). Apparently, this point was better grasped by the earlier Reformed theologians than subsequently; see M. Schneckenburger, *Vergleichende Darstellung des lutherischen und reformierten Lehrbegriffs* (Stuttgart: J. B. Metzler, 1855), 2:67-69, 80 and H. Heppe, *Dogmatik des deutschen Protestantismus* (Gotha: F. A. Perthes, 1857), 2:218; cf. H. Heppe, *Reformed Dogmatics*, trans. G. T. Thomson (London: George Allen & Unwin, [1950]), pp. 498f.

mediate context, vv. 20ff., Paul is concerned with the
adamic significance of Christ's resurrection): justifying
faith is worthless, if Christ has not been raised (cf. v. 14),
because a dead Christ is an unjustified Christ, and an unjustified Christ means an unjustified believer. Elsewhere
the appeal for justifying faith (Rom. 10:9) and even
justification itself (Rom. 8:34) is based primarily and
directly on Christ's resurrection or on Christ as resurrected.

I Timothy 3:16, Romans 4:25, and I Corinthians 15:17,
then, show that the enlivening of Christ is judicially
declarative not only, as we saw earlier, in connection with
his messianic status as son, his adoption, but also with
respect to his (adamic) status as righteous. The constitutive, transforming action of resurrection is specifically forensic in character. It is Christ's justification.

Sanctification

To speak of Christ's resurrection as his sanctification
may at first seem obviously wrong. Such language would,
of course, be improper, if the term were employed in its
customary sense, indicating the progressive ethical
renewal experienced by the believer. Paul's stress on the
obedience of Christ as well as his conception of Christ's
person precluded him from attributing to Christ the
depravity such moral renovation presupposes. However,
while Paul is certainly concerned with the progressive
transformation the believer must undergo and the reality
of his continuing struggle with sin (cf. esp. Rom. 7:14-25;
Gal. 5:13-26), he characteristically refers the vocabulary
of sanctification not to a process but to a definitive act occurring at the inception of the Christian life (Acts 20:32;
26:18; I Cor. 1:2; 6:11; Eph. 5:25; II Tim. 2:21; I Thess.
4:7; II Thess. 2:13).[148]

Nowhere does Paul discuss this definitive sanctification
more fully than in Romans 6:1ff., a passage figuring
prominently in his resurrection theology.[149] The controlling question in this passage, it will be recalled, is a
question that bears directly on sanctification: are
believers to continue to live in sin (vv. 1, 2b)? Also, the
factor basic not only to the negative answer given but also

---

148. Cf. Murray, "Definitive Sanctification," pp. 5f.
149. See above, pp. 44ff.

to the exhortation to progress in sanctification (vv. 12ff.) is that believers have died and been raised with Christ. By virtue of this involvement they are dead to sin, that is, alive to God (v. 11), alive from the dead (v. 13). Their freedom from the dominion and power of sin resides specifically in their having been raised with Christ. In other words, (definitive) sanctification is defined here expressly in terms of resurrection.

The pivotal role of the solidarity factor in this passage would appear to warrant the conclusion at this point that by analogy Christ's resurrection is his sanctification. Paul, however, relieves us of the necessity of relying solely on such an inference. In establishing the fundamental thesis of sanctification (v. 11), the immediately germane consideration is that Christ has died to sin and lives to God (v. 10).[150] The plain implication, then, is that prior to his resurrection (cf. v. 9) Christ was alive to sin. The preceding verse confirms this by stating that death (which is exponential of sin, cf. v. 23) *no longer* rules over him. It is likewise plain from verse 10 that his present life to God (subsequent to the resurrection) has its distinguishing character in contrast to his former life to sin. Further, this aspect of his resurrection, that is, his having died to sin and his living to God, provides the pattern for the experience of believers in their having died to sin and their living to God. "Even so" in verse 11 puts this parallel beyond question. For believers, having been raised with Christ is their (definitive) sanctification because Christ's resurrection is *his* sanctification.

As long as sanctification (whether definitive or progressive) is thought of exclusively as ethical renovation it will be difficult, if not impossible, to understand this element of Paul's thinking. For him the power of sin includes more than moral corruption. Specifically, σάρξ, with which hostility toward God and rebellion against his law (Rom. 8:7) and moral pollution (Gal. 5:19-21) are associated, specifies in an all-inclusive fashion the distinguishing character of the old aeon, the fallen preeschatological world order. Accordingly, sanctification embraces all that pertains to deliverance from the power

150. Cf. with the following remarks esp. Murray, *Romans*, 1:224f.

of the "flesh" understood in this comprehensive, aeonic sense. For Christ being made sin (II Cor. 5:21) involved him in being subject to the power of sin, that is, the dominion of "flesh." He not only bore the guilt of sin but in so doing he entered the sarkic order with a personal mode of existence commensurate with that order (Rom. 8:3) and thus was exposed to its suffering, weakness (II Cor. 13:4), and death. Consequently, as the point of his decisive breach with the old aeon and the ennervating power of "flesh," the resurrection is Christ's sanctification. Further confirmation for this conclusion, as well as the continuity in experience of Christ and believers, lies in the fact that (even) the (progressive) sanctification of the individual believer is defined expressly in terms of deliverance from the old age (Rom. 12:2; I Cor. 3:18; I Tim. 6:17; II Tim. 4:10; cf. Gal. 1:4; Titus 2:12).

Glorification

Passages like I Corinthians 15:42ff. and II Corinthians 3:17f.; 4:4-6, as well as the genetic association of glory with the Spirit,[151] show that the pneumatic transformation experienced at Christ's resurrection involves the final and definitive investiture of his person with glory. The organic tie between this aspect of the resurrection and the experience of believers emerges in the sequence of thought developed in Romans 8:29f.: glorification, standing at the end, is the realization of the predestined goal, conformity to the image of Christ. The image of Christ is specifically the image of the *resurrected* Christ (cf. esp. I Cor. 15:49). Accordingly, the plain implication is that what Christ is by virtue of his resurrection, believers will become at their resurrection; as his resurrection is his glorification, so their resurrection is their glorification.[152] This same implication is also present in Philippians 3:21: (at the resurrection, cf. vv. 10f.) Christ will transform the body of the believer so that it will be in

---

151. See above, p. 68.
152. Note the multiple expression given to the notions of solidarity and analogy in this verse. They are present not only in σύμμορφος and εἰκών but also in the conception of Christ as firstborn among many brothers. A valuable discussion of the bearing of these verses on Paul's resurrection theology is provided by Jervell, *Imago Dei*, pp. 271-284; cf. E. Larsson, *Christus als Vorbild. Eine Untersuchung zu den paulinischen Tauf—und Eikontexten* (Uppsala: C. W. K. Gleerup, 1962), pp. 302-307.

conformity to the body of (the resurrected) Christ, a body described expressly as the body of his (Christ's) glory (cf. II Cor. 3:18).

Conclusion

The resurrection of Christ is the resurrection of the last Adam; its significance resides in his solidarity with those for whom he purchased redemption. This is a fundamental determinant of Paul's resurrection theology. Our exploration of this point in this subsection, oriented to the notion of Christ's resurrection as his redemption, yields the following conclusions, decisive for further reflection on the structure of Paul's soteriology:

(1) The principal categories with which Paul explicates the salvation of the believer—justification, adoption, sanctification and glorification, are also used to expound the meaning of Jesus' resurrection. Putting the matter this way, however, partially obscures its real import. For in view of the solidarity between the experience of Christ and believers, in particular, the constitutive nature of the former, the direction of thought is rather that justification, adoption, sanctification, and glorification as applied to believers are derived from the significance of the resurrection for Christ.

(2) Justification, adoption, sanctification, and glorification as applied to Christ are not separate, distinct acts. Rather each describes a different facet or aspect of the *one act* of being raised from the dead.

RAISED WITH CHRIST

In Part II we saw that in dealing with the unity of the resurrection of Christ and the resurrection of believers, three organically related yet temporally distinct events must be taken into account: Christ's own resurrection from the tomb, the resurrection of the believer at the inception of Christian existence (the resurrection of the inner man), and the believer's future, bodily resurrection (the resurrection of the outer man). The second of these, as Romans 6:3ff. makes especially clear, is that aspect of being united (experientially) to the resurrected Christ so that in experience Christ's resurrection is the believer's. This realized aspect of the believer's resurrection experience we will now reexamine briefly in the light of conclusions reached in the preceding section.

First, contrary to the Reformed consensus,[153] in Paul the notion of having been raised with Christ does *not* correspond more or less exactly to the dogmatic conception of regeneration. Two passages make this clear.

The integrating theme of Ephesians 2:1-10 is "walking." This unit begins with the readers' former walk in trespasses and sins and ends with their walk in good works, so that a primary focus is the inward, subjective transformation effecting this radical reversal in conduct: this transition took place at the point God made them alive (existentially) with Christ (v. 5).

The experience of being enlivened with Christ, however, is further described as having been raised with him and having been seated in the heavenlies with him. The last two verbs most likely have an epexegetical reference to the first. At any rate, a real difference in meaning hardly exists between the first two, as if each describes a different event than the other. Accordingly, the expression "by grace you have been saved," interjected between two virtually identical verbs, is surely parenthetical (as indicated in all standard editions of the Greek text and almost every English translation), underscoring the gracious character of the initial experience of salvation described as enlivening, resurrection, and heavenly session with Christ. Consequently, when virtually the same expression is repeated several verses later (v. 8), there is no reason to suppose a different sense than in the earlier instance. The latter is best understood, in the informal, grammatically loose style often found in Paul's letters (cf. vv. 1ff.), as anticipating the former, so that "through faith," explicit in verse 8, is implicit in verse 5.

---

153. E.g., Hodge, *Systematic Theology*, 2:696, 703; 3:3, 5, 33f.; B. B. Warfield, "On the Biblical Notion of 'Renewal,'" *Biblical Doctrines* (New York: Oxford University Press, 1929), p. 458; Vos, *Eschatology*, p. 45; Kuyper, *Dictaten*, 4, Locus de salute: 76; Bavinck, *Dogmatiek*, 4:20f.; Berkhof, *Systematic Theology*, p. 465; H. Kuiper, *By Grace Alone. A Study in Soteriology* (Grand Rapids: Wm. B. Eerdmans, 1955), p. 46; cf. Murray, *Redemption—Accomplished and Applied*, p. 119. The view that being raised with Christ is a metaphor for regeneration (e.g., Kuyper: "beeld der wedergeboorte") is an inversion of Paul's way of thinking. As I Cor. 15:42ff. and Rom. 1:3f. (cf. Acts 13:33) make clear, the realistic counterpart to the natural process and birth is not new birth but resurrection. If the term regeneration is at all applicable to Paul's resurrection theology, *it* is the metaphor (cf. Titus 3:5).

This conclusion is supported by the parallel passage in Colossians 2:12f., the only other place where the first two of the main verbs in Ephesians 2:5f. are associated with each other and where Paul writes expressly that believers have been raised up with Christ "through faith."[154] If this exegesis is correct, then being raised with Christ is an experience with which faith is associated in an instrumental fashion and so, while including initial subjective renewal at the point of transition from wrath to grace, it is an experience clearly not identical with regeneration understood as prior to faith, as in the traditional Reformed doctrine.

Positively, as the parenthetical insertion in Ephesians 2:5 reflects, being raised with Christ, brought to bear there specifically on the initial ethical renewal of the individual sinner, has the broadest possible soteric dimensions. What these are is given with the meaning of Christ's resurrection; in view of the solidarity involved, being raised with Christ has the same significance for believers that his resurrection has for Christ. To be more exact, the notion that the believer has been raised with Christ brings into view all that now characterizes him as a result of having been joined to Christ *as resurrected*. It means that he has been justified, adopted, sanctified, and glorified with Christ, better, that he has been united with the Christ, who is justified, adopted, sanctified, and glorified, and so by virtue of this (existential) union shares these benefits.

A corollary of this conclusion is that everywhere Paul speaks of the believer's justification, adoption, sanctification, glorification (or any of the other benefits connected with these), there the more basic, underlying consideration is resurrection with Christ, that is, (existential) union with Christ as resurrected. Wherever he deals with the application of redemption to the individual believer, there the controlling factor is (experiential) involvement in Christ's resurrection and fellowship with the exalted Christ.

154. Regardless of the force of the following τῆς ἐνεργείας (objective genitive or genitive of source?), the instrumental character of faith here is plain. Note also that the above interpretation of Eph. 2:5f. does not depend upon an appeal to Col. 2:12f., although the apparent literary interdependence of the two passages (see above, p. 43) ought not to be depreciated.

It is difficult to overestimate the importance of this corollary for understanding both the basic structure and the details of Paul's soteriology. Little more than an indication of some of the primary and more significant implications can be given here.

(1) From its inception in the mid-nineteenth century, modern historical-critical study of Paul has found two basic strands in his soteriology (to employ the terminology adopted most frequently—the juridical and the ethical), and has maintained repeatedly that the relationship between these two lines constitutes a—if not *the*—fundamental problem for understanding Paul: how can what he says about God's forensic activity with respect to the sinner be harmonized with his teaching on subjective renewal? The sometimes complicated treatment of this problem can be passed over here, because, as usually posed, it is a false one.[155] It rests on the incorrect assumption that in Paul there are distinct strands of soteriological teaching, each involving separate divine acts, when in fact, because of the solidarity involved, what characterizes the redemption of Christ holds true for the redemption of the believer. As the justification, adoption, sanctification, and glorification of the former take place by and at his resurrection, so the justification, adoption, sanctification, and glorification of the latter take place in his having been raised with Christ, that is, in his having been united to Christ as resurrected. This means, then, that, despite a surface appearance to the contrary, Paul does not view the

155. A detailed survey of the debate up through the early decades of this century is provided by E. Wissmann, *Das Verhaltnis von* ΠΙΣΤΙΣ *und Christusfrömmigkeit bei Paulus* (Göttingen: Vandenhoeck & Ruprecht, 1926). Neugebauer orients his recent study to a brief summary (*In Christus*, pp. 9-17). The older liberal interpretation (in the interests of making Paul an exponent of an ethical idealism) stressed in varying degrees an antithesis between the two strands, viewing the ethical line as expressing Paul's real interest (e.g. H. Lüdemann, *Die Anthropologie des Apostels Paulus* [Kiel: Universitäts-Buchhandlung, 1872], pp. 159-173, 198ff.; H. J. Holtzmann, *Lehrbuch der neutestamentlichen Theologie*, 2nd ed. [Tübingen: J. C. B. Mohr, 1911], 2:125-131, 149-154). The subsequent trend has been toward a formal recognition of the priority of the forensic line, coupled, however, with its effective devaluation by treating justification as a metaphor (so, e.g., J. Jeremias, *The Central Message of the New Testament* (New York: Scribner's, 1965), pp. 51-70; E. Schweizer, "Dying and Rising with Christ," *New Testament Studies*, 14(1967-68):12-14; cf. Stuhlmacher, *Gerechtigkeit Gottes bei Paulus*, pp. 217-236.

156. Even if, for reasons overlooked here, it is correct to think of different acts rather than different facets of one act, there would still be no basis for trying to establish a sequence of causal priorities among the various acts. The only and decisive causality involved is being united to the exalted Christ in the fullness of his saving benefits.

justification, adoption, sanctification, and glorification of the believer as separate, distinct acts but as different facets or aspects of the *one act* of incorporation with the resurrected Christ. This is the natural inference from I Corinthians 1:30, regardless of the precise relationship of each conception to the others: "You are in Christ, who became to us wisdom from God, and righteousness and sanctification and redemption."[156]

This point may be pursued briefly by focusing on the perennial question of the relationship between justification and sanctification in Paul. Not only are the two not independent, unrelated interests, but it is not enough to say that sanctification (whether as definitive act or process) inevitably follows on the act of justification by a particular divine determination conjoining otherwise separable entities. Rather the two are indissolubly linked as different facets of the single act of being raised (incorporated) with Christ. The close connection between Romans 5 and 6 rests on the consideration that, having discussed the justification entailed by solidarity in Christ's resurrection (cf. 4:24),[157] Paul turns to treat the sanctification this solidarity also involves. This does not mean that Paul obscures the distinction between justification and sanctification. On the contrary, unlike many of his modern interpreters, he grasps too clearly the various needs created by sin to compromise either of these or any other of the manifold aspects of the redemption experienced so efficaciously in *resurrection.*[158]

157. While there is no explicit reference and very little direct allusion to the resurrection in chapter 5, the justifying righteousness and the justifying act should not be confused (cf. Murray, *Romans*, 1:385). Strictly speaking, the obedience, blood, and death of Christ which receive sustained emphasis in this chapter are the former, not the latter. The structure of the justifying act, then, will have to be understood in the light of 4:25 and the broader context of Paul's teaching, that is, in terms of resurrection (cf. v. 10). Accordingly, there is good reason for taking the genitive in the expression "justification of life" (v. 18) as appositional (*contra* Murray, ibid., p. 202; cf. Ridderbos, *Romeinen*, p. 122).

158. "Therefore we can never understand the depth and richness of Paul's message of justification by faith, if we divide justification and sanctification so that the former is involved only with the *guilt* of sin, the latter with the *power* of sin" (A. J. Venter, *Analities of Sinteties? 'N Analise van die Dilemma insake die Werklikheid van die Regverdiging* [Kampen: J. H. Kok, 1959], p. 199). This statement reflects a failure to grasp that the integration it properly seeks to express is provided by resurrection with Christ; hence unity can only be indicated by obscuring the distinction between aspects which Paul himself maintains. Similarly, in the debate between Karl Barth and Hans Küng, the slogan: "to declare righteous is to make righteous," short-circuits the apostle's point of view, unless resurrection is understood to be the common denominator.

At the same time, however, various considerations already adduced point to the conclusion that Paul does not view the justification of the sinner (the imputation of Christ's righteousness) as an act having a discreet structure of its own. Rather, as with Christ's resurrection, the act of being raised with Christ in its constitutive, transforming character is at the same time judicially declarative; that is, the act of being joined to Christ is conceived of imputatively. In this sense the enlivening action of resurrection (incorporation) is itself a forensically constitutive declaration.

This does not at all mean that Paul qualifies the synthetic character of the justification of the ungodly. The justifying aspect of being raised with Christ does not rest on the believer's subjective enlivening and transformation (also involved, to be sure, in the experience of being joined to Christ), but on the resurrection-approved righteousness of Christ which is his (and is thus reckoned his) by virtue of the vital union established.[159] If anything, this outlook which makes justification exponential of existential union with the resurrected Christ serves to keep clear what preoccupation with the idea of imputation can easily obscure, namely, that the justification of the ungodly is not arbitrary but according to truth: it is synthetic with respect to the believer only because it is analytic with respect to Christ (as resurrected). Not justification by faith but union with the resurrected Christ by faith (of which union, to be sure, the justifying aspect stands out perhaps most prominently) is the central motif of Paul's applied soteriology.

That the subjectively transforming elements of saving experience are aspects of having been raised with Christ is plain from passages like Ephesians 2:5f. and Romans 6:3ff. and does not need to be argued further. In addition to the remarks just made on justification, the following verses serve to underscore that forensic elements are likewise facets of being joined to the resurrected Christ. Galatians 3:26f. makes clear that the adoption in Christ received through faith (cf. 4:5) derives from being bap-

159. Cf. Edwards, *Works*, 4:71: "What is real in the union between Christ and his people, is the foundation of what is legal; that is, it is something that is really in them, and between them, uniting them, that is the ground of the suitableness of their being accounted as one by the Judge."

tized into Christ (putting on Christ), that is, from being joined to Christ. According to Romans 8:34, justification depends not simply on an action in the past experience of the believer but on his present relation to the person of the resurrected Christ (cf. I Cor. 15:17).[160]

Further, recognizing that forensic and transforming elements are integrated as aspects of the single act of being united to the exalted Christ points the way to an unforced interpretation of I Corinthians 6:11: "but you were washed, but you were sanctified, but you were justified in the name of the Lord Jesus Christ, and in the Spirit of our God." On the view that the initial experience of redemption consists of a series of judicial and pneumatic acts each distinct from the others, this declaration is permanently unintelligible. A tolerable sense is obtained only by concluding that the association of the Spirit with justification requires giving the latter a causative sense[161] (something it does not have even remotely elsewhere in Paul), or by recourse to the syntactically arbitrary expedient of distributing the prepositional phrases chiastically, that is, construing the first with the last verb, the last with the first two verbs.[162] If, however, one brings to bear the redemptive-historical considerations developed later in the same letter in the context of 15:45, the result is a smoothly flowing, rhetorical combination expressing something of the fullness of redemptive benefit enjoyed by virtue of having been united (note the aorist tenses) to the resurrected Christ who *is* the Spirit (cf. 1:30).[163]

(2) The organic inseparability of the future, bodily resurrection of believers from the realized aspect of being raised with Christ appears to involve the important structural implication that for Paul the justification, adoption, sanctification, and glorification of the believer are future as well as present.[164] This implication cannot be explored here except to point to some of the evidence for

---

160. Cf. Schäder, *Die Bedeutung des lebendigen Christus*, pp. 175f.; Vos, *Eschatology*, pp. 153f., n. 9.
161. Cf. Murray, *Romans*, 1:349f. Note, however, Murray's own reservation that a causative sense is not "beyond question" (p. 350).
162. Vos, "Eschatology and the Spirit," p. 237, n. 36.
163. If, as is most probable, "you were washed" is a reference to baptism (Grosheide, *I Cor.*, pp. 141f.; cf. Acts 22:16), this is an indication of the close affinity of this verse with Rom. 6:3ff.; Gal. 3:26f. and Col. 2:11ff.
164. Cf. esp. Vos. *Eschatology*, pp. 42–61.

the future aspect of justification (Gal. 5:5) and adoption (Rom. 8:23) as well as sanctification-glorification (Phil. 3:21), and to observe that this no more compromises the definitiveness and irreversibility of the justification (and so forth) already realized than future resurrection compromises the definitiveness and irreversibility of resurrection with Christ already experienced.

In this light the suggestion is also worth considering that the *catena* of Romans 8:29f. is best understood in terms of this tension between resurrection as present and future: the predestined goal, realized in successive steps, is conformity to the image of the Son, that he might be first-born among many brothers. This end is hardly any other than the adoption said expressly in verse 23 to be the resurrection of the body (cf. I Cor. 15:49, Phil. 3:21). Accordingly, it is not reading into the text but rather bringing out the underlying structure to paraphrase verse 30 as follows: those whom God predestined to resurrection with Christ (defined in terms of the aspect of adoption; cf. Eph. 1:5), these he also called (into fellowship with the resurrected Christ, I Cor. 1:9); and whom he called, these he also has already raised with Christ (defined in terms of the aspect of justification); and whom he has already raised with Christ, these he also will raise with Christ (defined as glorification; cf. II Cor. 4:14).

Conclusion

In bringing this study to a close, some indication can be given of the bearing our findings have on the set of broader issues raised in the introduction:

(1) What is the distinguishing concern of Paul's soteriology? Is his controlling interest the historical accomplishment of redemption or its individual application? While both are present as clearly distinct, yet inseparable concerns, a major conclusion of this study is that a redemptive-historical outlook is decidedly dominant and determinative. We have found that the resurrection of Christ is *the* pivotal factor in the whole of the apostle's soteriological teaching. Not only is the resurrection (as it is constitutive of the ascension and heavenly session) the climax of the redemptive history of Christ; it is also that from which the individual believer's experience of redemption derives in its specific and distinguishing character and in all aspects of its inexhaustible fullness. For in transforming Christ's person, the resurrection and no other event (or consideration) constitutes him as life-giving Spirit to those joined to him. It and no other event inaugurates the new age, the eschatological aeon, into which others are brought, so that he might be "firstborn among many brothers."

To be more specific, we have found that redemption, both in the experience of Christ as the last Adam and in that of believers, is defined expressly in terms of resurrection (with Christ) and in the final analysis consists in the state of being raised (with him). So thoroughly does this redemptive-historically conditioned solidarity control Paul's thinking that the primary categories he employs to explicate the realization of redemption in the life history of the believer are derived from the significance of resurrection for Christ himself. Justification, adoption, sanctification, and glorification all have a common redemptive-historical, resurrection-qualified origin and complexion. Further, as with Christ so with believers, these are not distinct acts but different facets of a *single act*, in the case of the latter, the act of being raised with Christ, that is, being united to Christ as resurrected.

(2) What dogmatic consequences follow for thinking controlled, as in Paul, by his redemptive-historical outlook? Some important doctrinal implications can be tentatively indicated by exploring the comparison, suggested particularly by the discussion toward the end of Part III (pp. 114–136) between the structure of Paul's resurrection soteriology and the traditional dogmatic conception of the *ordo salutis*.[1]

Such a comparison is, of course, a study in its own right, requiring, among other things, a survey and careful analysis of voluminous dogmatic materials. Consequently, the partial and provisional character of the observations made here should be underscored. Further, the comparison intended is apparently problematic methodologically, particularly among Reformed theologians. Jan Ridderbos, for one, has rejected as unworthy of scientific Reformed study of the Bible, the attempt "to answer an essentially dogmatic question by exegesis of a small portion of Scripture" and without reference to the history of dogma.[2] Berkouwer warns against the "one-sidedly Pauline" approach that can result when one is gripped by his letters, observing that a tendentious appeal to Paul in support of a theological distortion of the gospel is by no means an imaginary danger—as the example of Marcion makes so glaringly obvious.[3] And the opinion of Herman Bavinck is that especially where the *ordo salutis* is concerned, dogmatics is neither interested in simply stringing together biblical concepts nor required to employ biblical terms in precisely the same sense they have in Scripture.[4]

---

1. Again, *ordo salutis* here refers to the application of redemption in the life history of the individual sinner.
2. "Over de Heils-zekerheid," *Gereformeerd Theologisch Tijdschrift*, 40 (1939): 338; cf. p. 336: "The method of wanting to answer dogmatic questions solely on the basis of studying Scripture without adequately reckoning with confessional documents and dogmatic developments, is to be rejected as biblicistic."
3. G. C. Berkouwer, *Faith and Justification*, trans. L. B. Smedes (Grand Rapids: Eerdmans, 1954), pp. 62f.
4. *Dogmatiek*, 3:597.

Certainly these viewpoints contain a necessary warning, and the pertinent methodological questions require more attention than they have received in this study. Nevertheless, there are sufficient grounds to warrant the proposed comparison. Two considerations are primary: (i) Most decisive is the line of argument explored in Part I,[5] namely, that by virtue of the (ecclesiastically qualified) redemptive-historical context common to Paul and subsequent generations of the church, there is no objection in principle to viewing his writings as containing dogma in the proper sense of the word. Reference to the letters of Paul is reference to the history of dogma. Apparently, then, Paul's doctrine is commensurate with the subsequent dogmatic production of the church, so that, where the textual data permits, a Pauline structure may be compared with a later dogmatic structure.

(ii) Beyond this, it remains the case that the biblical basis for the central elements in the usually accepted *ordo salutis*—calling, faith, justification, adoption, sanctification, and glorification, is, in each instance, either almost exclusively or at least characteristically Pauline. If, for reasons it deems sufficient and necessary, dogmatics gives these terms a different content than Paul and relates them to each other differently, then at the very least it should be apprised of these differences, especially when it cites Paul for support. The force of this observation is compounded by the further consideration, likewise indisputable, that the structure, the internal alignment, in short, the *ordo*, of the traditional *ordo salutis* is customarily and primarily based on Romans 8:29f., so far as an appeal to Scripture is concerned.[6] At issue here is the leading and regulating function of exegesis (biblical theology) with reference to systematic theology.[7]

A comparison between the structure of Paul's soteriology and the traditional *ordo salutis* discloses three principal differences:

(a) The traditional *ordo salutis* lacks the exclusively eschatological air which pervades the entire Pauline soteriology.

---

5. See esp. pp. 26f.
6. E.g., Berkhof, *Systematic Theology*, p. 416; Murray, *Redemption—Accomplished and Applied*, pp. 100-103.
7. See above, p. 26.

(c) Unlike the traditional *ordo salutis* Paul explicates the inception of the application of redemption without recourse to the terminology of regeneration or new birth understood as "a communication of a new principle of life."[13] As I have tried to show above, the passage in Ephesians 2:1ff., usually appealed to in support of this conception, has in view rather an experience with which faith is associated instrumentally.[14]

So far as the term "regeneration" (παλιγγενεσία) in Titus 3:5 is concerned, the following three observations need to be considered: (i) This usage is beset with linguistic and syntactical difficulties such that it can hardly serve as a direct or firm basis for the dogmatic conception of regeneration.[15] (ii) The only other occurrence of the term in the New Testament (Matt. 19:28) has clearly eschatological force. That this gospel usage refers to future, cosmic renovation, while in Titus 3:5 the term describes the present experience of the individual believer, does not exclude a connection between the two.[16] On the contrary, within the resurrection soteriology developed by Paul, as Romans 1:4 and especially I Corinthians 15:45ff. make clear, the present experience of the believer is not only eschatologically conceived but cosmically qualified. It is existence in the new creation, the age-to-come. The relevance of this consideration for understanding Titus 3:5 appears from the fact that the term "renewal" (ἀνακαίνωσις), closely associated there with "regeneration," refers in its only other occurrence in Paul (Rom. 12:2) to the present renewing of the believer's mind in pointed contrast with conformity to "this age." In view, then, is renewal which is nothing less than transformation within and according to the norms of

13. Hodge, *Systematic Theology*, 3:33; "the principle of new life . . . implanted in man" (Berkhof, *Systematic Theology*, p. 469); "implanting of the seed of new life" (Kuyper, *Dictaten*, Locus de salute, 4:70); "infusion of the principle of new life" (Bavinck, *Dogmatiek*, 4:100).
14. See above, pp. 128f.
15. Some of these difficulties are recognized by Warfield ("On the Biblical Notion of 'Renewal,'" p. 454), although he does feel that a "narrower connotation" approaching the dogmatic conception "seems tolerably clear." Cf. Ridderbos (*Paul*, p. 227, n. 45), who disputes the derivation of the dogmatic conception from this text; J. Dey, ΠΑΛΙΓΓΕΝΕΣΙΑ—*Ein Beitrag zur Klärung der religionsgeschichtlichen Bedeutung von Tit 3, 5*, NA, 17, 5 (Münster: Aschendorff, 1937), p. 135.
16. Cf. Vos, *Eschatology*, p. 50; F. Büchsel, *TDNT*, 1:688. Ridderbos (*Paul*, pp. 226f.) stresses the eschatological character of the usage in Titus 3:5.

the age-to-come. Also, if "washing" (λουτροῦ), on which "regeneration" is directly dependent in Titus 3:5, refers to baptism,[17] then what Romans 6:3ff. (cf. Gal. 3:27; I Cor. 12:13) teaches concerning baptism as a sign and seal of incorporation with the resurrected Christ, and so the implications of that incorporation, will have to be brought to bear here. All told, then, the use of "regeneration" in Titus 3:5 is to be explained as a subordinate element in Paul's resurrection theology. In particular, as it describes what the believer has already experienced, it is an aspect of the experience of being raised with Christ, that is, the experience of being joined to the resurrected Christ.[18] (iii) This usage, by virtue of its lone occurrence, is hardly a distinguishing mark of Paul's soteriology.

This last observation points to a real difference, a basic incongruity. Even though it has thought improperly in terms of a sequence of separate acts, Reformed soteriology has taken over with exemplary faithfulness those individual doctrines of Paul which bear on the inception of the application of redemption. Precisely because of this fidelity, however, the inclusion of that factor which more than any other has come to distinguish it, namely its doctrine of regeneration, works as something foreign and extraneous in comparison with Paul's *ordo*.

This does not at all mean that Paul jeopardizes what the Reformed doctrine of regeneration has sought to safeguard. Nothing could be more alien to his teaching than the notion that the sinner in and of himself possesses some spark of life or the capacity for faith. Paul's sustained emphasis on the Spirit as the sole source and communicator of life in the soteric sense, his constant

---

17. For a recent survey of interpretive opinion on this point and a decision in favor of a reference to baptism, see George W. Knight, III, *The Faithful Sayings in the Pastoral Letters* (Kampen: J. H. Kok, 1968), pp. 95f., 109-111.

18. In the closely related conception found in II Cor. 5:17 an eschatological and cosmic connotation is likewise present. Both Vos (*Eschatology*, pp. 46-48) and Ridderbos (*Paul*, pp. 45f.) emphasize this point. The former favors the rendering "a new creation" to the more usual "a new creature"; the latter writes, "When he speaks here of 'new creation,' this is not meant merely in an individual sense ('a new creature'), but one is to think of the new world of the re-creation. . . ." Note also the qualifying reference to resurrection in verse 15. Similarly "the new man" described in Col. 3:10ff. (cf. Eph. 4:24) is the one who has been raised with Christ, vv. 1-4.

Or, to put it the other way around, the former point of view amounts to a definite de-eschatologization of Paul's outlook. For him soteriology *is* eschatology. All soteric experience derives from solidarity in Christ's resurrection and involves existence in the new creation age, inaugurated by his resurrection. As Romans 8:30 reflects,[8] the present as well as the future of the believer is conceived of eschatologically. This understanding of present Christian existence as an (eschatological) tension between resurrection realized and yet to be realized is totally foreign to the traditional *ordo salutis*. In the latter, justification, adoption, sanctification (and regeneration) are deprived of any eschatological significance and any really integral connection with the future. Eschatology enters the *ordo salutis* only as glorification, standing at a more or less isolated distance in the future, is discussed within the locus on "last things."

(b) Nothing distinguishes the traditional *ordo salutis* more than its insistence that the justification, adoption, and sanctification which occur at the inception of the application of redemption are separate acts.[9] If our interpretation is correct, Paul views them not as distinct acts but as distinct aspects of a single act. The significant difference here is not simply that Paul does not have the problem that faces the traditional *ordo salutis* in having, by its very structure, to establish the pattern of priorities (temporal? logical? causal?) which obtains among these acts. Even more basic and crucial is the fact that the latter is confronted with the insoluble difficulty of trying to explain how these acts are related to the act of being joined *existentially* to Christ. If at the point of inception this union is prior (and therefore involves the possession in the inner man of all that Christ is as resurrected), what need

---

8. See above, p. 134.
9. So, e.g., Murray, *Redemption*, pp. 97f.; *Romans*, 1:27 (n. 21), 321 (n. 62); Berkhof, *Systematic Theology*, p. 416; Bavinck, *Dogmatiek*, 3:596–604. That this is the plain assumption of the other leading Reformed dogmaticians (Kuyper, Hodge, Shedd) can hardly be disputed. The question whether these acts and others (regeneration, faith) in their mutual relations are always only logically (causally) distinct or in some instances may also be temporally distinct need not be entered into here except to note that the apparently popular tendency in Reformed circles to view regeneration as temporally prior to faith (and justification) is an indication of how thinking is regulated by the notion of a plurality of acts. Even a dogmatician like Bavinck speaks of the possibility of the temporal priority of regeneration to faith (*Dogmatiek*, 4:100). See also above, p. 130, n. 156.

is there for the other acts?[10] Conversely, if the other acts are in some sense prior, is not union improperly subordinated and its biblical significance severely attenuated, to say the least?[11] The structure and problematics of the traditional *ordo salutis* prohibits making an unequivocal statement concerning that on which Paul stakes everything in the application of redemption, namely union with the resurrected Christ. The first and, in the final analysis, the only question for the Pauline *ordo* concerns the point at which and the conditions under which incorporation with the life-giving Spirit takes place. And the pointedness of this question is not blunted nor is its centrality obscured by introducing considerations deriving from solidarity with Christ in the design and accomplishment of redemption. So, for example, Paul writes with unrelieved sharpness concerning the Ephesian Christians that, prior to being joined existentially to the resurrected Christ (2:5f.), they were "without Christ" (v. 12), "far off" (v. 13), "children of wrath, even as the rest" (v. 3), although, as he himself fully recognizes, they were chosen in Christ (ἐν αὐτῷ) before the foundation of the world (1:4).[12]

10. Note that the progressive character of sanctification and the future character of the other aspects are *not* at issue here.

11. John Murray (*Redemption*, pp. 201-213) has given what is perhaps the best summary treatment of the doctrine of union with Christ. His insistence, however, that (in its existential aspect) union is not to be coordinated with the other acts in the application of redemption but underlies them and binds them together (p. 205), is not and cannot be made intelligible in terms of the *ordo* of separate acts with which he is working.

In the past, Reformed dogmatics has not recognized the dilemma posed above simply because, against the background of its covenant concept, it has tended to equivocate on the notion of union with Christ, using union (being contemplated one) with Christ in the design and accomplishment of redemption (Bavinck: "the objective *unio mystica*") as working capital in the area of application. See, e.g., A. A. Hodge, "The *Ordo Salutis*; or Relation in the Order of Nature of Holy Character and Divine Favor," *The Princeton Review*, 54(1878):305-321, esp. 316-318 and J. Macleod, *Scottish Theology* (Edinburgh: The Banner of Truth Trust, 1974), pp. 124-127, 129f.; cf. also Bavinck, *Dogmatiek*, 3:519-523, 4:100, 198, 235, passim; Berkhof, *Systematic Theology*, pp. 447-450. C. A. Briggs (*Theological Symbolics* [Edinburgh: T. & T. Clark, 1914], pp. 366-371) poses the dilemma in a sharp and unsympathetic fashion. For a brief discussion of the un-Pauline character of this equivocation, see above, pp.53ff.

12. Primarily because he feels that the centrality of Christ, in the application of redemption is obscured, Berkouwer has largely broken with the traditional *ordo salutis*; cf. esp. *Faith and Justification*, pp. 25-36. R. H. Bremer (*Herman Bavinck als Dogmaticus* [Kampen: J. H. Kok, 1961], p. 360) gives the following assessment of Berkouwer's program of dogmatics: "His own framework of discussion as a whole . . . involves an unexpressed criticism of the *ordo* of Bavinck and Kuyper."

stress on faith as an expression of this life (e.g., I Cor. 2:4f.; I Thess. 1:5; II Cor. 3:3 in connection with I Cor. 3:5; II Cor. 4:13), as well as his insistence on the absolute, all-embracing, unqualified antithesis between the natural and spiritual man (I Cor. 2:14f.), between the "flesh" and the Spirit (Romans 8:5ff.; Gal. 5:16ff.)—all prohibit attributing to him such a conception. The origin of the believer's faith does not lie in himself but in the calling of God, which in its irrevocable efficacy and power is life-giving and creative (Rom. 4:17; 11:29; Eph. 1:18-20; II Tim. 1:9). Yet this calling only realizes its enlivening function in the act of establishing fellowship with Christ (I Cor. 1:9), the life-giving Spirit, apart from whom there is neither life nor justification nor adoption nor sanctification nor any other saving reality; and for the effecting of this union, faith is the necessary instrument (Gal. 3:26f.). It would be wrong to an extreme to qualify the deadness mentioned in Ephesians 2:1ff. Yet the transition from wrath to grace, the passing from death to life described there, takes place through faith (v. 5 in connection with v. 8; cf. Col. 2:12). It would appear, then, that in Paul's soteriology there is a correlation between Christ as life-giving and the sinner as life-receiving (i.e., Christ-receiving) which carries back to the very point of inception of salvation, a correlation which characterizes the *single act* of being joined to Christ.

This correlation is no doubt subject to various distortions and every effort must be made to guard against them. However, the question posed here is whether the notion of a distinct enlivening act (causally or temporally) prior to the initial act of faith serves this end or is not rather itself a distortion of Paul's viewpoint.

This question brings us to the limits of this study. Only a careful, balanced consideration of the broader biblical-theological context and the course of dogmatic developments will be able to reach a final judgment on the compatibility of the Reformed doctrine of regeneration with Paul's soteriology. It does seem in order, however, to suggest that in its discussion of soteric renewal, dogmatics ought to apply in a developed and all-inclusive fashion the observation already made by Warfield on the relevant teaching in the New Testament epistles:

There is certainly synergism here; but it is a synergism of such character that not only is the initiative taken by God, but the Divine action is in the exceeding greatness of God's power, according to the working of the strength of His might which He wrought in Christ when He raised Him from the dead (Eph. 1:19).[19]

19. "On the Biblical Notion of 'Renewal,' " p. 451. Note also the remarks of Vos on the pattern of thought in Phil. 3:8-11: "And that it is not impossible for Paul to hold up the resurrection as a goal to be striven after, appears from the fact that he here plainly so represents the spiritual resurrection, which elsewhere he views quite as much as the bodily resurrection under the aspect of an absolute act or gift of God. . . . It is at one and the same time a divine grace and a Christian attainment" (*Eschatology*, pp. 257f.). This "spiritual resurrection," taken here by Vos primarily as a reference to the process of sanctification, is elsewhere (esp. p. 45) clearly viewed by him as Paul's way of describing regeneration ("the soteric experience, whereby believers are introduced into a new state").

Selected Bibliography

Bavinck, H. *Gereformeerde Dogmatiek.* vols. 3, 4, 4th ed., Kampen: J. H. Kok, 1930.

Bultmann, R. *Theology of the New Testament.* vol. 1, trans. K. Grobel, New York: Charles Scribner's Sons, 1951.

Deissner, K. *Auferstehungshoffnung und Pneumagedanke bei Paulus.* Leipzig: A. Deichert, 1912.

Hamilton, N. Q. *The Holy Spirit and Eschatology in Paul.* Scottish Journal of Theology Occasional Papers, No. 6, Edinburgh: Oliver and Boyd, 1957.

Hermann, I. *Kyrios und Pneuma. Studien zur Christologie der paulinischen Hauptbriefe.* Studien zum Alten und Neuen Testament, 2, München: Kösel-Verlag, 1961.

Hodge, C. *A Commentary on the Epistle to the Romans.* Grand Rapids: Louis Kregel, 1886.

Kramer, W. *Christ, Lord, Son of God.* SBT, 50, trans. B. Hardy, Naperville, Ill.: Alec R. Allenson, 1966.

Kuyper, A. *Encyclopaedie der Heilige Godgeleerheid.* vol. 3, Kampen: J. H. Kok, 1909.

Murray, J. "Definitive Sanctification." *Calvin Theological Journal*, 2 (1, April 1967):5-21.

_____. *The Epistle to the Romans.* NICNT, 2 vols., Grand Rapids:Eerdmans, 1959, 1965.

_____. *Redemption—Accomplished and Applied.* Grand Rapids: Eerdmans, 1955.

Ridderbos, H. *Aan de Romeinen.* CNT, Kampen: J. H. Kok, 1959.

_____. *Paul: An Outline of His Theology.* Grand Rapids: Eerdmans, 1975, trans. J. R. DeWitt, of *Paulus. Ontwerp van zijn Theologie.* Kampen: J. H. Kok, 1966.

Schäder, E. *Die Bedeutung des lebendigen Christus für die Rechtfertigung nach Paulus.* Gütersloh: C. Bertelsmann, 1893.

Schweizer, E. *Erniedrigung und Erhöhung bei Jesus und seinen Nachfolgern.* ATANT, 28, Zürich: Zwingli-Verlag, 1955.

Vos, G. *Biblical Theology: Old and New Testaments.* Grand Rapids: Eerdmans, 1959.

———. "The Eschatological Aspect of the Pauline Conception of the Spirit." *Biblical and Theological Studies* by the Members of Faculty of Princeton Theological Seminary, New York: Scribner's Sons, 1912, pp. 209-259.

———. *The Pauline Eschatology.* Grand Rapids: Eerdmans, 1961.

Warfield, B. B. "The Christ that Paul Preached." *Biblical Doctrines*, New York: Oxford University Press, 1929, pp. 233-252 (=*The Expositor*, 8th series, 15(1918):90-110; *The Person and Work of Christ*, ed. S. C. Craig, Philadelphia: The Presbyterian and Reformed Publishing Company, 1950, pp. 71-90).

Scripture Index

Genesis
2:7   79f., 82, 84, 87
49:3   38

Exodus
4:22   37
23:16   36
23:19   34, 36

Leviticus
2:14   36
23:10   34
23:17   36
23:20   36

Numbers
15:20f.   34
18:8, 11f.   34
18:12f.   36
18:30   34
30:3ff.   118

Deuteronomy
18:4   34
21:17   38
26:1f.   34
26:2, 10   34

I Samuel
7:14   114

Nehemiah
10:36f.   36

Psalms
2:7   63, 114
50(51):11   104
88(89):26   114
88(89):27   37, 114

Isaiah
63:10f.   104

Ezekiel
44:30   36

Matthew
1:24   63
2:13   63
9:25   64
12:41   64
19:28   140

Mark
2:12   63
3:26   64
11:30   84

Luke
7:14   64
10:25   64
11:8   63
11:32   64
22:22   117

John
2:19-22   65
6:63   86
10:17f.   65
11:29   63

Acts
2:23   117
2:24   116
6:9   64
10:42   117
11:29   117
13:16-37   113f.
13:30   62

13:33   37, 62f.,
    113f., 118, 128
13:37   62
17:3   65
17:26   117
17:31   62, 117
20:30   64
20:32   124
22:16   133
24:10ff.   62
26:18   124
26:23   111

Romans
1:1-7   98
1:1   105f.
1:3f.   98-114,
    117f., 119-22, 128
1:4   37, 68f.,
    89, 140
1:11   85
1:16   105
1:23   97
1:32   81, 104
2:5ff.   62
2:7   69f.
3:20   107
3:24f.   115
4:5   121
4:17   44, 63, 142
4:24   62f., 131
4:25   63, 98,
    122-24, 131
5:10   81, 131
5:12ff.   36, 45, 81
5:14   82
5:15   81
5:17   81
5:18   131

5:18f.	116
6:1ff.	41, 44-52,
53-55, 57, 78, 124f.,	
127, 132f., 141	
6:4	62f., 68f., 93
6:9	63
6:10	116, 125
6:12	61, 79
6:16	81
6:19	70
6:20-23	81
6:21	81
6:23	81, 116, 125
7:4	51f., 58, 63
7:5	107
7:6	52, 69, 93
7:14	85
7:14-25	124
7:22ff.	61
7:24	79
8:2	69, 81, 93, 96
8:3	48, 70,
106, 116, 126	
8:4ff.	70, 103,
108, 142	
8:6	69, 81, 93
8:7	125
8:9-11	66-68, 73
8:10	69, 93
8:10f.	79
8:11	44, 61-63,
68f., 86, 110	
8:13	81, 103
8:15	35
8:15f.	71f.
8:23	35, 114,
118f., 121, 134	
8:26	70
8:26f.	72
8:29	38, 48, 50,
65, 95, 101	
8:29f.	126, 134, 137
8:30	138
8:32	106
8:34	63, 72, 91,
124, 133	
9:5	106, 109
10:9	62f., 124
11:12	81
11:14	107

11:16	35
11:29	142
12:2	61, 109,
	126, 140
12:4f.	45
13:11	63
14:8f.	38
15:1	70
15:13	69
15:19	69
15:30	72
16:5	35
16:25f.	24

I Corinthians

1:2	124
1:9	51, 134, 142
1:20ff.	107f.
1:24	73
1:26	107
1:29	107
1:30	73, 114,
	131, 133
2:3f.	70
2:4	69, 86, 142
2:5	69, 142
2:6-16	109
2:10-15	85f.
2:14	108
2:14f.	120, 142
3:1	108, 120
3:3	70, 108, 120
3:5	142
3:18	107, 126
3:19	108
5:5	103
6:2	62
6:11	72, 124, 133
6:14	62f., 68f.
6:20	115
7:23	115
7:31	109
10:3f.	94
10:11	29
11:7	97
11:15	97
11:32	62
12:1	85
12:4ff.	72
12:13	45, 51, 71,

	141
12:27	45
14:1	85
15:4	63f.
15:12-19	40f., 64
15:12	63
15:14	63, 124
15:15	62, 64
15:16	63
15:17	63, 123f.,
	133
15:18	35f.
15:19	47
15:20-23	34-36, 39,
	88, 124
15:20	36f., 39, 63
15:22	44, 66, 78
15:32	64
15:35f.	78
15:40	97
15:42-49	70, 78-92,
	97, 107f., 120,
	126, 128
15:43	69f.
15:43f.	68f.
15:44	68
15:45	36, 47, 66,
68f., 92f., 96f., 105,	
110f., 133, 140	
15:47-49	36
15:49	95, 101,
	126, 134
15:51	105
15:52	64
15:53f.	79
15:54	69
15:56	81
16:15	35

II Corinthians

1:12	109
2:15f.	81
3:1—4:6	92-97, 109
3:3	142
3:6	69, 86
3:7f.	81
3:8	68
3:9	81
3:10	68
3:11	81

3:17	68, 92-97,
3:17	68, 92-97,
	105, 109f., 126
3:18	48, 68,
	101, 127
4:4	68, 109, 126
4:6	68, 101, 126
4:10f.	61f., 79
4:11	107
4:13	40, 142
4:14	40f., 61-63,
	68, 134
4:16	61f.
4:18	109
5:2	84
5:10	62
5:14f.	57
5:15	63, 66, 141
5:17	43, 141
5:21	116, 121, 126
7:1	103
10:3	107, 109
10:4	70
12:9	70
13:3f.	70
13:4	68f., 110, 126
13:13	72

Galatians

1:1	63
1:4	42, 126
2:1-10	99
2:16	107
2:19	45
2:19f.	41, 52f.
2:20	107, 109
3:3	70
3:13	115, 121
3:26f.	45, 132f.,
	142
3:27	45, 50, 141
4:4	106
4:5	115, 121, 132
4:6	71f.
4:13	70
4:13f.	62, 107
4:21—5:1	96
4:23	107
5:5	134
5:12ff.	108, 124
5:13	96

5:16	70
5:16ff.	96, 103,
	142
5:19ff.	108, 125
5:25	69
6:1	85
6:8	69, 81, 103

Ephesians

1:3	85, 90
1:4	50f., 139
1:5	134
1:7	115
1:13	70
1:14	114
1:17ff.	63
1:18	69, 142
1:19	68, 142f.
1:20	91, 142
1:22f.	39
2:1-10	41-43, 46,
	51, 128f., 140, 142
2:3	139
2:5	45, 62
2:5f.	41-43, 45,
	53, 78, 132, 139
2:6	48, 62, 91
2:10	43
2:11-13	51
2:12	139
2:13	43, 139
2:14	109
3:16	61, 69
4:4ff.	72
4:15f.	39
4:22-24	49
4:24	141
4:30	72f., 114
5:14	65
5:19	85
5:23	39
5:25	124
6:5	107
6:12	85

Philippians

2:6-8	116
2:6-11	98, 112,
	118
2:6	106
2:7	48

2:9	64, 91f., 121
3:3	70
3:3f.	103
3:8-11	143
3:10f.	126
3:21	48, 68,
	126, 134
4:7	61

Colossians

1:9	85
1:11	69
1:15-18	36-39
1:18	36-39, 101
1:22	107
2:11-13	45, 133
2:12	45, 48, 62,
	64, 68, 142
2:12f.	41, 43f.,
	78, 128
2:13	62
2:20	44
3:1	41, 43f.,
	49, 64, 141
3:1–4:6	44
3:4	69
3:9f.	49
3:10ff.	141

I Thessalonians

1:5	69, 142
1:10	23, 63
2:16	104
4:7	124
4:14	41, 64f.
4:16	64f.
5:19	70

II Thessalonians

1:8	62
1:9	69
2:13	124

I Timothy

2:6	115
3:16	68, 98, 109,
	112, 119-22, 124
6:17	126

II Timothy

1:9	142

1:10	70	2:14	115	5:5	114, 118
2:8	63f.	3:5	140f.	6:5	109
2:11	45				
2:17f.	78	**Philemon**		**I Peter**	
2:21	124	16	107	3:18	86, 112,
4:10	126				116, 121
		Hebrews			
Titus		1:5	114, 118	**II Peter**	
2:12	126	4:7	117	3:16	27

Author Index

Alexander, J. A., 113
Althaus, P., 47, 81

Bachmann, P., 80-83, 92
Barrett, C. K., 122
Barth, K., 54
Barth, M., 15, 122
Bavinck, H., 12, 128, 136, 138-40
Becker, J., 104
Bengel, J. A., 64
Berkhof, L., 12, 128, 137-40
Berkouwer, G. C., 15, 56, 115f., 136, 139
Bertrams, H., 71
Best, E., 51, 56
Betz, O., 12
Bornkamm, G., 37, 39
Bouma, C., 119f.
Braun, F.-M., 104
Bremer, R. H., 139
Briggs, C. A., 139
Bruce, F. F., 37, 109
Büchsel, F., 89, 140
Bultmann, R., 35, 62, 71, 73, 98, 106, 122

Calvin, J., 86, 100, 103, 113, 115, 117, 120
Charles, R. H., 104

Dahl, M. E., 65
Davies, W. D., 73
Deissner, K., 84, 89f.
Delling, G., 34, 100
Dey, J., 140
Dodd, C. H., 99
Dunn, J. D. G., 77

Eadie, J., 42
Edwards, J., 123, 132
Ellis, E. E., 80

Fairbairn, P., 120
Fletcher, V. H., 15

Gaffin, R., 26
Greijdanus, S., 101, 113, 122
Griffiths, D. R., 92
Grosheide, F. W., 36, 42, 65, 68f., 79, 81-84, 86f., 95, 97, 113, 119f., 133
Grundmann, W., 47, 69
Gundry, R. H., 119f.
Guntermann, F., 59, 89
Guthrie, D., 37
Güttgemanns, E., 115

Haenchen, E., 113
Hahn, W. T., 54, 58
Hamilton, N. Q., 87, 90, 96
Headlam, A. C., 103, 110
Hendriksen, W., 42, 43, 118-20
Heppe, H., 123
Hermann, I., 35, 39, 71, 89, 92
Hodge, A. A., 139
Hodge, C., 12, 42, 65, 81, 84, 87, 93-97, 100-103, 106, 111f., 117, 120, 128, 138, 140
Holtzmann, H. J., 130
Hughes, P. E., 61, 93f., 95f.

Jeremias, J., 78, 90, 119f., 130
Jervell, J., 89f., 126
Jewett, R., 106

Käsemann, E., 29, 36, 39, 70f., 98
Kelly, J. N. D., 120
Kennedy, H. A. A., 62
Kertelge, K., 91
Kline, M., 27
Koch, R., 37, 74, 90
König, A., 37f.
Knight, G. W., 141
Kramer, W., 62, 98, 111
Kühl, E., 103
Kuiper, H., 128
Kümmel, W., 12
Kuss, O., 53, 60, 122
Kuyper, A., 12, 20-22, 25, 27, 128, 138, 140

Lagrange, M.-J., 110
Larsson, E., 126
Lengsfeld, P., 27
Lietzmann, H., 104, 118
Lohmeyer, E., 38
Lüdemann, H., 130

Machen, J. G., 54
Macleod, J., 139
Michaelis, W., 38
Michel, O., 67, 98, 110f., 117, 122
Milligan, G., 34
Molitor, H., 62, 65
Morris, L., 87, 115
Moulton, J. H., 34
Murray, J., 12, 26, 43-45, 47-49, 51, 53-55, 57f., 62-65, 67, 72, 78, 85, 99, 101, 104-106, 110, 113, 116f., 121-24, 126, 128, 131, 133, 137-39

Neugebauer, F., 54, 130
Nygren, A., 111f.

Oepke, A., 64
Oudersluys, R. C., 90

Plummer, A., 68, 84, 92, 94
Poythress, V. S., 98
Procksch, O., 103

Ramsey, A. M., 15
Reumann, J., 98

Ridderbos, H., 13-14, 16, 35, 37-39, 42f., 47-49, 53-58, 61f., 67, 78, 84f., 101, 104, 106, 110, 117, 119f., 122, 131, 140
Ridderbos, J., 136
Robertson, A. T., 68, 84
Robinson, H. W., 56f.
Robinson, J. A. T., 58

Sanday, W., 103, 110
Sasse, H., 60
Schäder, E., 91, 133
Schildenberger, J., 73
Schmidt, K. L., 118
Schmitz, O., 69
Schnackenburg, R., 41, 47, 52
Schneckenburger, M., 123
Schweitzer, A., 28f., 35, 59
Schweizer, E., 71, 73, 98, 106, 111, 118, 120, 130
Scroggs, R., 80, 83
Sevenster, G., 111
Shedd, R. P., 56
Shedd, W. G. T., 12, 138
Simpson, E. K., 42
Smeaton, G., 100
Sokolowski, E., 69, 100, 110
Stalder, K., 73
Stanley, D. M., 15
Stuhlmacher, P., 91, 130

Tannehill, R. C., 48, 56
Thornton, L. S., 57f.
Thüsing, W., 48
Turner, N., 84

Van Daalen, D. H., 64
Van Leeuwen, J. A. C., 42f.
Venter, A. J., 131
Versteeg, J., 77, 87
Vos, G., 12-14, 16, 19-23, 25f., 28f., 35, 59-62, 64f., 67, 70, 73, 82-84, 89-91, 97, 100, 104, 108-12, 117, 121f., 128, 133, 140f., 143

Wagner, G., 53f.
Warfield, B. B., 12, 24f., 28, 71, 100-106, 109, 111f., 115, 128, 140, 143
Weiss, J., 34, 80, 84

Whiteley, D. E. H., 15
Windisch, H., 41, 92, 94
Wissmann, E., 130

Zahn, T., 22f.
Zerwick, M., 84

Subject Index

Adoption, 117-19, 130f., 132f.

Biblical theology, 11f., 19f., 26f., 137

Christ
  ascension of, 91f.
  and the Holy Spirit, 87, 89, 95-97, 110f.
  as the second Adam, 36, 39, 60, 66, 85, 135
  union of believers with, 50-52, 53-58, 73, 129-34
Corporate personality, 55-58

Eschatology
  and the Holy Spirit, 90f., 110-12
  and soteriology, 13f., 59, 82, 90f., 137f.

"Flesh," 106-109

Glorification, 126f., 130f.

Holy Spirit
  and Christ (*see* Christ)
  as a divine person, 70-73
  and eschatology, 90f., 110-12

Imputation, 132

Justification, 119-24, 131-33
  and sanctification, 131

Ordo salutis, 11, 13f., 29, 43, 52, 77, 94, 136-43

Redemption, accomplished and applied, 59
Regeneration, 128f., 140-43
Resurrection of believers
  anthropological explication, 60-62
Resurrection of Christ
  as his adoption, 117-19
  and his ascension, 91f.
  and his death, 115f.
  as his glorification, 126f.
  in the history of Reformed dogmatics, 11f.
  as his justification, 119-24
  as his sanctification, 124-26
Resurrection of unbelievers, 62

Sanctification, 124-26
  and justification, 131

Theology
  nature of, 23-25
  relation of biblical theology and systematic theology, 26f., 137

Union with Christ (*see* Christ)